THE SAFETY OF THINGS

Considerations for keeping human, physical and digital assets safe – the critical infrastructure perspective

For my beloved wife, Dasha, who motivates me to be better and do better every single day.

Family and friends, of course. Wherever you (or I) may be, you are always on my mind.

Mentors and advisors over my lifetime, too numerous to list, you may or may not know who you are or the impact you had. Even the awful ones and the crappy experiences. I learned lots of lessons and just know I am grateful.

And to you, dear reader, because time and attention are our most important assets, so I'm flattered that you have chosen to expend some of both on this book.

Thank you all.

Foreword

The importance of infrastructure lies in the eye of the beholder. In our just-in-time world, many of us overlook the delicate web that sustains our way of life, failing to grasp how quickly our comfortable lifestyles could falter. It seems that, at times, the lessons of COVID-19 are neither learned nor retained.

In this modern world, critical infrastructure forms the foundation of society's daily life. It encompasses the systems and services essential to our communities, economies, and even personal well-being. From the roads and bridges we travel on, to the electricity powering our homes, the water flowing from our taps (faucets), and the digital networks connecting us - these elements make up a vast, interconnected system that we often take for granted.

For generations, people's essential needs were simple yet profound: clean running water, reliable energy, food, a job, and safe transportation. These have always been, and remain, the lifeblood of any functioning society. Access to these basics ensures health, security, and the ability to grow. For many worldwide, these needs are still paramount, and the infrastructure that provides them is life-sustaining.

However, as societies evolve, so do their expectations for infrastructure. The digital age has introduced a new set of needs. What was once a luxury - communication across distances, instant access to information, and the ability to work or learn from anywhere - is now indispensable. In today's world, the loss of a stable Internet connection can be as disruptive as a power outage or water shortage might have been for previous generations. Modern dependence on digital infrastructure means that for many, the absence of Wi-Fi is more than a trivial inconvenience; it's a genuine barrier to daily functioning.

This book explores the critical infrastructures supporting these diverse needs, from the tangible to the intangible. It asks critical questions about how societies adapt their infrastructure to meet both present and future demands. It examines the balance between ensuring no one is left behind - particularly those still struggling to access basic services - and advancing the systems that support our increasingly digital world. Above all, it considers how we can build resilient, secure, adaptable infrastructure that meets the needs of all citizens, from those for whom clean water is essential to those who find themselves unmoored by a momentary loss of connectivity.

This is a book about the invisible threads that bind us together - threads we rarely notice but that, when broken, remind us just how dependent we are on the systems underpinning our way of life.

This definition goes beyond the obvious. In a world grappling with climate change, sustainability becomes central to securing a safe future for the generations to come. For instance, a safe school is, to us, an essential part of societal safety.

This book is a guide on how to deliver critical infrastructure successfully, and keep it safe. It weaves a golden thread of experience and grounded capability. I commend it to you all.

Captain Philip S (Paddy) Parvin Royal Navy Retired

Former Chief Engineer and Safety Director of the Royal Navy Submarine Forces 2019-2022

The Safety of Things

Considerations for keeping human, physical and digital assets safe – the critical infrastructure perspective

Contents

FOREWORD 5

INTRODUCTION 9
    Why Am I Writing This Book? 9
    Who Are We, and How are We Qualified? 10
    So, What Do I Mean by "Things"? 11
    Objectives and Goals of the Book 13
    Historical Context and Evolution of Safety Measures ... 15
    The Importance of Critical Infrastructure Safety 16
    Legal and Ethical Considerations in Infrastructure Safety 19

CHAPTER 1 - THREAT ASSESSMENT AND RISK MANAGEMENT 21
    Conducting Comprehensive Risk Assessments 21
    Physical Security Assessment 21
    Cybersecurity Assessment 24

CHAPTER 2 - PHYSICAL SECURITY MEASURES 29
    Technology and Physical Security 29
    Non-Crunchy Technology 29
    Crunchy Technology 31
    Which brings us to the next chapter, cybersecurity for critical infrastructure. 35

CHAPTER 3 - CYBERSECURITY FOR CRITICAL INFRASTRUCTURE 36
    Educating People on Cyber Safety 37
    Protecting Operational Technology (OT) 38
    Cloud Security 41
    IoT and IIoT 43
    Responding to Cyber Threats and Incidents - IRP 45
    AI and Cybersecurity 51
    Considerations for AI 53

CHAPTER 4 - CYBER-PHYSICAL CONVERGENCE 55

WHAT IS IT?..55
KEY CONSIDERATIONS – THE DOWNSIDE..55
KEY CONSIDERATIONS – WHAT YOU NEED TO DO 57
IS IT WORTH IT?...59

CHAPTER 5 - PEOPLE 61

BACKGROUND CHECKS 61
BEHAVIORAL ASSESSMENT 63
CONTINUOUS MONITORING AND BEHAVIORAL REASSESSMENT....64
PROMOTING MENTAL HEALTH AWARENESS 65
CREATE A SUPPORTIVE CULTURE. 66

CHAPTER 6 – PROCESS...69

CREATING COMPREHENSIVE CRITICAL INFRASTRUCTURE SAFETY
POLICIES 69
EMERGENCY PREPAREDNESS AND RESPONSE 73
PPP BEST EXAMPLES 77

CHAPTER 7 - DESIGNING SECURE INFRASTRUCTURE FACILITIES 83

LAYERED SECURITY ZONES: 87
CONVERGENCE AND LAYERS (INTEGRATION OF CYBER AND
PHYSICAL SECURITY) 90

CHAPTER 8 – SAFETY CONSIDERATIONS TODAY 92

NUCLEAR..92
MILITARY BASES – SMART BASES 98
SCHOOLS...102

CHAPTER 9 – THE FUTURE 112

PEOPLE 112
PROCESS..114
TECHNOLOGY...115
GOVERNANCE, RISK, AND COMPLIANCE (GRC) 117
QUANTUM 119

CHAPTER 10 – CONCLUSION 124

Introduction

Why Am I Writing This Book?

Well, hello, and thanks for picking up this book. A little about me: I'm a 50-something Brit living in America. I'm a bit of an introvert, which stems from being British and our self-depreciating culture. Which makes living in America pretty strange at times for me. My sense of humour (the correct spelling, I'll revert to US "English" spelling and grammar from now) is also very British, so forgive me if that finds its way into some of the chapters in this book. I can't help it.

(As an aside I am writing another book about the differences and similarities between British and American cultures, look out for that it's properly funny.)

So anyway, if you want to know a bit about who I am and what I'd doing here, that's below. If not, skip the next paragraph or two.

I've had a fabulous career travelling the world consulting on (some might say 'fixing') cool technology projects. I'm a recovering network engineer and project manager by trade, but also gained an MBA along the way which means I speak both technology and business. And Risk, having performed too many assessments over the years. I came to the US over 12 years ago to help get The Cosmopolitan of Las Vegas over the line. I loved being the CTO, I had a fabulous team (you know who you are), but that one nearly killed us all! That's a whole other book. I fell in love with the culture of the US, the work ethic, the weather (being British, less rain is good), the business climate, and my wife, Dasha. Dasha persuaded me to share ownership and take the role of CEO in her cybersecurity company - Stealth-ISS Group® Inc., and relocate to the US permanently, and see what we could build. That's another story involving Smart Cities, major sporting events, and helping countless companies to either not get hacked, or save them when they were. We also won some company and individual awards.

Along my journey I've encountered loads of smart people and disparate technologies, and they are all interconnected in my head. I'm a visual guy, so imagine a mind map with a thousand blobs and tens of thousands of connections. In 3D. Anyway, it occurred to me one day while watching yet another in the seemingly endless news stories about school shootings, that it might be an idea to bring those blobs and lines (technologies, people and processes) together, with a touch of governance, to build a service that goes part or all of the way to solving that problem. Then I thought, well, why stop at schools?

So, I started a new company, Total Security Global Inc. (TSG), to bring the right people and technologies together with the initial aim of helping schools to save lives, and also working with some of our partners on various state and country-wide security initiatives (including some places you wouldn't typically go on vacation to). We're also building some cool technology, but that's for another book. With the widespread introduction of AI, the increasing threats to critical infrastructure, the lowering cost of sensors, the convergence of physical and cybersecurity, and with the US finally recognizing the benefits of Smart Cities and the components thereof, the timing is perfect.

Who Are We, and How are We Qualified?

Back to some of the smart folks I've met along the way. My stellar Advisory Board comprises the following experiences and capabilities which I hope you'll agree give us a legitimate voice when it comes to the Safety of Things – all of the assembled not only help steer the company but also played a part in reviewing, critiquing, and writing sections of this book, and for that I am eternally grateful:

- Paddy Parvin: Nuclear Safety and Advisory – Royal Navy Captain, Retired, Former Chief Engineer and Safety Director of the Royal Navy Submarine Forces 2019-2022
- Len Jessup: Ex-Dean of multiple Business Schools and Universities (US), Technology Startup Advisor (International), bestselling author
- Anonymous: Tiers 1 and 2 Special Forces (UK)
- Jared Sparhawk: Security Systems Architect and Integrator (International)
- Tom Clegg: Smart Cities Architect (Abu Dhabi, Singapore, Azerbaijan)
- Dasha Davies: Cybersecurity Consulting and MSSP President and CISO (International), author, wife, legend
- Dean Inniss: $Bn Business Leader (US)

Each and every one has had a say in this book, and I thank them sincerely for their time and belief in what I'm trying to achieve with TSG. You can find them via LinkedIn, or I'm happy to make an introduction.

So, What Do I Mean by "Things"?

By 'Things' I am mostly talking about human, physical and data assets, and, at the meta or macro level, the things that are made of those things – specifically critical infrastructure such as smart cities, schools, military bases, etc.

Put another way, officially speaking there are 16 critical infrastructure sectors, as defined by CISA (the Cybersecurity and Infrastructure Security Agency) whose "assets, systems, and networks, whether physical or virtual, are considered so vital to the United States that their incapacitation or destruction would have a debilitating effect on security, national economic security, national public health or safety, or any combination thereof":

- Chemical – converting raw materials into products
- Commercial Facilities – large crowds of people – shopping, business, entertainment
- Communications – the enabler across all critical infrastructure
- Critical Manufacturing – metals, machinery, electrical equipment
- Dams – includes hydro-electric power generation
- Defense Industrial Base (DIB) – research and development of weapons systems
- Emergency Services – law enforcement, fire and rescue
- Energy Supply
- Financial Services
- Food and Agriculture
- Government Services – facilities and education
- Healthcare - protects all sectors of the economy from hazards such as terrorism, infectious disease outbreaks, and natural disasters
- Information Technology
- Nuclear Reactors, Materials and Waste
- Transportation – aviation, highways, maritime, railways
- Water and Wastewater

All of those 16 sectors are comprised of physical, human and digital assets. So, by keeping those safe, we keep our 3 asset classes safe, and vice versa.

Harm comes in many guises – physical, economic, reputational to name but a few. We also have to consider safety not just from a personal perspective but also as a member of a wider community where more than one person could be harmed – schools, sporting events, towns, city, state, country. There are many examples of harm in all of those locations.

12

So, back to the mind map with blobs and lines, as mentioned in my head mine is in 3 dimensions and not 2! Especially because I layer in personal data and all the other non-human assets that, if compromised, could harm you in non-physical ways. Again, not just as individuals but as part of a community. Here I'm thinking about critical infrastructure – what if your community power grid was hacked and disabled? You might not be able to cook or keep your food cold, pay your bills or work from home on the Internet, buy gas for your vehicle which would stop you from going to work. What if your local hospital was unable to perform life-saving surgeries? The consequences of any of those could cause you harm in some way. Best case you'd be inconvenienced for a while.

By the way, when it comes to threats to critical infrastructure, not all are externally generated (insider threat is more of an issue than you might think), nor are they all intentional – accidents can have the same effects on citizens as malicious activity. More on that later.

I'll try to cover all of the above, and more, in the following pages. My problem is there are so many rabbit holes I'd love to take you down, to keep this book to a reasonable length I'm having to keep concepts and ideas at a relatively high level. If you, dear reader, do have questions or need the detail, my contact details will be in the book somewhere and I encourage you to reach out. Either way, I hope you enjoy the book and might even be willing to leave some feedback – positive or negative – for this is how we all learn and grow.

Objectives and Goals of the Book

You could read the book from start to end, or use specific chapters as reference material. Either way, my objective is to share a little of what I've learned in as entertaining a way that a topic like this can be. It's not meant to be an encyclopedia, and it's certainly not meant to be perfect or all-encompassing. I'm sure some very important topics are not included. But my hope is that it encourages people to 'think wider' – maybe add some dots and lines to those already present in your head.

One more thing to bear in mind. This book was written in 2024. If you've arrived at it in 2030, assuming we're all still here, I suspect much written here could be obsolete. Who knows, I may even update it every couple of years. When quantum goes mainstream, I'll definitely update it then.

This book aims to provide a relatively comprehensive understanding of the importance of critical infrastructure safety and offer practical guidance for enhancing the resilience and security of essential systems, for the eventual safety of us citizens. The primary objectives include:

Education. To inform you, the public/citizens, about the critical importance of infrastructure safety and the potential consequences of neglect or accident. From the CISA list above, you'll agree this is not a small task.

Providing Best Practices. To offer actionable insights and best practices for assessing risks, implementing safety measures, and responding to emergencies. To plagiarize an often-used management consulting term, we'll be looking at People, Process and Technology. And GRC (Governance, Risk Compliance) too.

Encouraging Collaboration. To provoke discourse, add fuel to existing (but maybe not joined-up) conversations, and promote collaboration among communities, government agencies, and private sector organizations to enhance the safety and resilience of critical infrastructure. The citizen's voice is often not heard, I hope this book gives rise to some different or more pointed questions that could be asked.

Fostering Innovation. To highlight the role of technological innovation in improving critical infrastructure safety, and by association safety of citizens, and encourage the adoption of cutting-edge solutions in a holistic, effective, efficient way. Aligned with people, processes and governance as mentioned earlier.

Historical Context and Evolution of Safety Measures

The importance of critical infrastructure safety has evolved over time, driven by technological advancements, changing threat landscapes, and lessons learned from past incidents. These tend to have a knock-on effect on governance requirements and even laws, which for the most part is a good thing. And of course, people (training) and continuous improvement in the form of evolving processes.

Early Developments. Initially, safety measures focused on physical security and accident prevention. For example, early power plants and water systems were designed with basic physical safety protocols to prevent tampering, mechanical failures and accidents.

Post-9/11 Era. The terrorist attacks on September 11, 2001, marked a significant turning point. Governments around the world recognized the need for enhanced security measures to protect critical infrastructure from terrorism. This led to the establishment of specialized agencies and frameworks dedicated to infrastructure protection. Yes, this has been inconvenient (think airport scanners and how much less enjoyable airline travel is these days), but you have to agree has been a good thing overall.

Modern Challenges. The advent of digital technology and the Internet of Things (IoT) introduced new challenges and opportunities. Cybersecurity has become a central concern as critical infrastructure systems have become increasingly interconnected and reliant on digital networks. Can you think of any business that doesn't use technology as a core part of business operations? Most if not all IT systems have some kind of third-party connection for support purposes. Consider the Vegas casino that was hacked via a fish tank thermometer. Consider the Target hack in 2013 – there are countless examples of entities being compromised via these connections including in 2021 when hackers cut off the supply of oil in America's largest fuel pipeline, "one of the most significant attacks on critical national infrastructure in history".

At a personal level think about your home. Yes, that smart microphone is very useful, but do you really want a live microphone in your house connected to the Internet? Is the convenience really worth the risk? What's wrong with dimming the lights yourself? When you invite a digital voice assistant into your home, you're inviting a device that records and stores things you say, which will be analyzed by a computer, and maybe by a human (even though they say they don't). You won't always know what happens with those recordings. Best case you receive more targeted marketing (like we all want more of this?), worst case, well, use your imagination.

Climate Change. In recent years, the growing impact of climate change has highlighted the need for resilient infrastructure that can withstand extreme weather events, rising sea levels, and other environmental threats. Whether you believe these changes are largely driven by human activities, or as a direct result of solar activity, the resulting changes in climate have far-reaching implications for the environment, ecosystems, and human societies. After Hurricane Sandy, New York City implemented a comprehensive resilience plan, including flood protection measures, infrastructure upgrades, and emergency preparedness initiatives. The plan focused on protecting vulnerable neighborhoods, enhancing building codes, and investing in green infrastructure. Basically, your plans have to evolve as the word turns. But you do need a plan.

The Importance of Critical Infrastructure Safety

This might sound obvious, but it's worth underlining why all this is so important. The safety and resilience of critical infrastructure is paramount for maintaining the daily operations of society and ensuring the safety of us, the public. The consequences of unsafe or compromised infrastructure can be severe and far-reaching, including:

Economic Disruption. The failure of critical infrastructure can lead to significant economic losses. For instance, a power outage can halt industrial production, disrupt financial transactions, and cause widespread economic instability. Think about the Suez Canal blockage in 2021 and the affect this had on the global supply chain. The world was already reeling due to Covid-19, but the ramifications of delays to the delivery of key manufacturing components affected a multitude of industries. And pure economics dictates that lack of supply causes prices to rise. Car and truck prices in 2023, anyone?

Public Health Risks. Unsafe infrastructure can directly impact public health. Contaminated water supplies, for example, can lead to disease outbreaks, while compromised healthcare facilities can impede access to medical services during emergencies. In March 2024, the White House warned that cyberattacks are hitting water and wastewater systems "throughout the United States" and state governments and water facilities must improve their defenses against the threat.

National Security Threats. Critical infrastructure is often a target for terrorism and other malicious activities, including nation states. Disabling these systems can undermine national security, weaken defense capabilities, and create vulnerabilities that adversaries can exploit. On Jan 31, 2024, FBI Director Christopher Wray testified before Congress, explaining how Chinese government hackers were trying "to find and prepare to destroy or degrade the civilian critical infrastructure that keeps us safe and prosperous." These hackers, Wray continued, "are positioning on American infrastructure in preparation to wreak havoc and cause real-world harm to American citizens and communities, if or when China decides the time has come to strike." As early as 2009, Chinese and Russian hackers infiltrated America's electrical grid, installing malware that could be used for future attacks. A 2017 hack of the Wolf Creek nuclear power plant in Kansas was later revealed to be the work of Russian hackers, as was a 2022 attack on an international food company, which temporarily closed all of its meatpacking plants in the United States. The warrior of today is a script kiddy in a regime basement where the West is the enemy. Seriously, our foes are building hacking universities, and their intent is to be able to disable us with keyboards, not missiles.

On an arguably less impactful scale, our company Stealth-ISS was involved in the Russian hack on a global winter sporting event in South Korea in 2018. We were instrumental in fixing the games infrastructure just before opening ceremony was televised. That's another book I should write. Point is, it's real, and it's happening in front of our very eyes all the time.

Social Instability. The disruption of essential services such as electricity, water, transportation and even schools can lead to social unrest, erode public trust in government institutions, and create chaos in communities. The safety and functionality of critical infrastructure are closely intertwined with social stability. When infrastructure is compromised, it can exacerbate existing social tensions and lead to further instability. On August 14, 2003, a major power outage affected parts of the Northeastern and Midwestern United States and Ontario, Canada, leaving an estimated 55 million people without electricity. The blackout lasted up to two days in some areas and caused significant disruptions in transportation, communication, and healthcare services. The immediate social impact included panic, gridlock, and increased crime rates in some cities.

Environmental Damage. Failures in infrastructure such as oil pipelines, chemical plants, or nuclear facilities can lead to environmental catastrophes, affecting ecosystems, wildlife, and human health for generations. In April 2014 (to date), the city of Flint switched its water supply from Detroit's system to the Flint River to save money. Due to inadequate treatment and lack of corrosion control, lead leached into the water supply, exposing residents to toxic levels of lead.

Legal and Ethical Considerations in Infrastructure Safety

We have to take a moment to bring in yet another dimension! Ensuring the safety of critical infrastructure also involves a complex interplay of legal and ethical considerations. Governments and organizations must navigate these aspects to develop effective governance frameworks, safety policies and practices.

Regulatory Compliance. There are numerous laws and regulations designed to protect critical infrastructure, and these evolve (for the better of citizens) over time. These include safety standards, environmental regulations, and cybersecurity laws. Compliance with these regulations is essential to mitigate risks and avoid legal penalties. Some industries are governed by more than one set of regulations, for example hospitals in the US that accept credit card transactions have to adhere to HIPAA and PCI-DSS, plus data privacy regulations like GDPR (or equivalents) becoming more and more real.

Ethical Responsibility. Beyond legal obligations, governments, organizations, and individuals have a moral obligation to protect and preserve the essential systems and services that society depends upon. These responsibilities extend beyond legal requirements and are grounded in the principles of fairness, justice, and the common good. The ethical responsibility for ensuring the safety of critical infrastructure is built on several key principles: Duty of Care, Justice and Equity, Transparency and Accountability, and Sustainability.

There are ethical challenges that should not be underestimated; allocation of scarce resources, communicating risk, and balancing privacy and security. Who decides? Think about Hurricane Katrina that hit New Orleans, and the very public arguments about equitable access to resources to support all affected communities, including vulnerable populations.

Privacy Concerns. Implementing security measures, particularly in cybersecurity, must balance safety with privacy rights. Organizations must ensure that protective measures do not infringe on individual privacy and civil liberties. For example, much as you might want to identify the students and faculty in a school for safety reasons, from the individual perspective would you want to be tracked everywhere you go? Much as George Orwell was quite prophetic in his novel 1984 back in the day, this is not China.

(GPT Trivia: The city currently with the most surveillance cameras per head of population is Taiyuan, China, with around 115 cameras per 1,000 people. Outside of China,

London ranks highly with approximately 65 cameras per 1,000 people, and Hyderabad in India has about 83 cameras per 1,000 people. Being a Londoner, I can tell you I'm not sure the city is any safer – cameras don't instill a sense of security, and they seem to have replaced actual police officers on the streets. Criminals just seem to have moved to areas with less cameras. Anyway, I digress.)

Corporate Governance. Effective governance is crucial for infrastructure safety. This is really about risk management and making sure companies do the right thing (legally and ethically) which includes establishing clear lines of responsibility, promoting transparency, and ensuring accountability to stakeholders including we, the people.

Chapter 1 - Threat Assessment and Risk Management

Conducting Comprehensive Risk Assessments

You'll find this mentioned a few times in this book, but like any good journey, your satnav/GPS needs to know where you are before it can plot a course to your intended destination. For me, this starts with an assessment. I'll talk about facilities, buildings, entities, bases and even cities. But these can be used almost interchangeably because they boil down to a common set of 'starter' questions, the answers to which we then use to drill into the specific context we are focused on, like a school. There are three main assessments at play here, and they overlap a bit:

Physical Security Assessment

There are many frameworks you could choose from if you wanted to do this yourself. NIST, ISO, DOE PSS, many industry specific ones. We find the best approach is to take all the parts relevant to your operating context from all the different frameworks, and tailor an assessment specifically for you. Not a sales pitch, just the way we do things. Let me give you an example – your company may take credit cards, and so is therefore in scope for PCI-DSS certification. What's wrong with that you might ask? Well, from experience, PCI-DSS is only interested in the bit of your operation that handles credit cards. Everything else is 'out of scope'. So, if only 10% of your company infrastructure handles credit cards, you might get your shiny PCI-DSS certification, but 90% of your company could still be vulnerable because it was never assessed. As we say all the time, being compliant doesn't necessarily make you secure.

Anyway, in advance of our visit, and aside from our own research on the facility and its operations, we request names, roles and training qualifications of any key security personnel and key stakeholders, and confirm if background checks were/are performed before being hired. We usually conduct our own research too. We ask for schematics and drawings of security systems, access control, and any policies relating directly to security, emergencies/alarms, incident response, that type of thing. It's also useful for us to know of relationships and communication tools and procedures with emergency services, community associations (think PTA), the church, and even links with adjacent buildings (could you share CCTV footage for example?).

Once we understand the scope (is it just a building, or is the surrounding land in scope also) we start with analysis of the exterior, which gives us fuel for interviews with the security team on site. Things to consider would be proximity to other things, like roads and buildings – could someone easily drive a half ton truck through your front entrance or park it nearby with a bomb for example? (on April 12, 2024, a man crashed a stolen semi-trailer truck into a Texas Department of Public Safety office in Brenham, Texas, killing two people and injuring twelve others). Could a sniper have line of sight from and adjacent building or crane? (Think Las Vegas Mandalay Bay 2017, and more recently (2024) the assassination attempt on Donald J Trump at a political party rally).

We assess the current state of physical security – gates, access control systems, fences, guards, cameras, lighting (often times we return at dark for this), and security signage.

During our walkabout we would remove any badges and note if we were challenged and check later if we were spotted on camera. We look for people/vehicular choke points. We look for other physical vulnerabilities such as access to waste disposal or HVAC systems, storage of hazardous materials, and make a note of critical and high value physical assets and how they are protected.

We identify muster points, and also regular hazards such as lakes or wooded areas. We even determine the direction of the prevailing wind, which is useful if your state is susceptible to forest fires. In some cases, we even get on the roof to assess aircraft flight paths and proximity to airports.

As you'd expect, next is the internal assessment. Access control, ability to tailgate, alarm systems, internal structure material, sight lines and any restricted areas. I have to share an example at this point. We performed this exercise recently at a relatively well-known but new school in the US, of which the superintendent was rightly insanely proud. Light, airy, natural daylight, open spaces, glass sided classrooms – a beautiful, contemporary building and learning environment. Problem being an armed assailant could easily drive through the front doors from the main road out front, and open fire at will. The kids would have no place to hide in the classrooms, and running away would take too long given the lines of sight throughout the property. To add insult to injury there was a metal fabrication workshop near the entrance with bottles of very flammable gas used for welding. It doesn't take much imagination to work out what could happen next.

The Industrial Internet of Things (IIoT) deserves a special mention here. This refers to interconnected sensors, instruments, and other devices networked together with computers' industrial applications, including manufacturing and energy management. This connectivity allows for data collection, exchange, and analysis, potentially facilitating improvements in productivity. It's mostly covered in the cybersecurity assessment below because it's data and network related, however there are physical security considerations – what does the entire system look like, and how it is protected? For example, if you have some kind of data center, how is that protected? What does access control look like? Do you have backups and redundancy, and a disaster recovery plan? Fire suppressant?

Once we've had a good look around, we meet with the head of security and whomever they want to bring along. We learn about how their security systems operate, and the plans, processes and procedures behind emergencies, visitor management, and take a look the coverage and recording capabilities of their CCTV system.

Then we go away and write the report. And combine it with the cybersecurity report below, and use both to deliver a comprehensive risk assessment.

Cybersecurity Assessment

As mentioned previously we tailor these assessments specifically for the requestor, and take the relevant parts of cybersecurity frameworks like NIST and ISF, industry frameworks such as SOC2 and NERC CIP, and industry best practice. We ask about any particular pain points that need to be focused on, and whether any major projects are being considered or are in the process of being delivered. This is because cybersecurity assessments are delivered at a point in time, but company operations evolve and change every day, this is why industry best practice suggests having a new assessment every year, or after a major change to your operations – in fact some industry frameworks mandate this. Think about CMMC (Cybersecurity Maturity Model Certification), which is the mandate from the US DoD for their supply chain contractors to protect American ingenuity and national security information. Their position is that cybersecurity must be a day-to-day consideration and part of the culture of your company and rigorously assessed by a qualified third party, not a self-assessment performed once a year at best. Ever wondered why new Chinese jet fighters look exactly like American ones? This is why CMMC is about to get very real for 300,000 companies in the DIB (Defense Industrial Base).

We ask a ton of questions about how your technology is set up and connected, what it comprises of, how it's connected internally and also to the outside world, and what security tools you may have in place already.

Then it gets intense. We meet with all major stakeholders in your facility, from IT through HR to Legal, because we typically have 300-400 detailed questions about people, process and technology that need to be answered for us to get a full picture of where you are. With HR we want to understand staff training and awareness, from Legal we want to know about risk management and company policies, and from IT we go through everything from network configuration to security tool configuration.

Fun anecdote – you could argue that a company's CISO (Chief Information Security Officer) is really a paid scapegoat – when bad things happen, they are the first to go. Well, given the churn of CISOs in the marketplace, as with any senior position when you join a company you want to make your personal mark before you have to leave. This can take many forms but in a lot of cases a CISO will argue to deploy their favorite security tool. Over time we see a lot of very similar security tools in companies, all quite expensive and none of them particularly well configured. In the past we have helped companies consolidate their tools, get them working properly and save them a ton of money on licenses they no longer need. Win-win, right?

We perform a thing called a vulnerability scan. We check all your systems to see if they have had their security patches applied. Think of it this way, every now and again you receive a message to upgrade your phone because someone has found a way to get at your data or cause things to fail. Well, OT (Operational Technology) and Industrial Control Systems follow the same process. Tame hackers all over the world try to break systems and get paid if they are successful. It's called bug bounty. The manufacturer then plugs that hole and releases the change as an update to your systems. But you still have to apply it (unless you subscribe to automatic updates, but this isn't always a good idea). They're called vulnerabilities, and we can scan for them. Bad actors have a list of all the vulnerabilities over time, and scan your systems to see if you've fixed them. If not, they can gain access and do bad things.

Next up we take those vulnerabilities and try to exploit them. That's a penetration test. Basically, we gather some tame hackers and let them loose, with varying levels of access, to your internal and externally facing networks to see a) if they can traverse your network and find the critical stuff, and b) whether they can elevate their privileges to be able to do anything they want. We test your Wi-Fi, gather and crack passwords, and can perform code reviews if for example you have written an application that you or your customers can access from the Internet.

This all sounds a bit like a huge risk, but we have to subscribe to a thing called Rules of Engagement (RoE). Here, you tell us what we can test, when we can test, and how far we can go. Industrial Control Systems and VOIP (Voice over IP) systems are typically very fragile, they break very easily. So, in the RoE we typically have to tread very carefully around these and in some cases do not touch them at all. Which is a bit counter intuitive but if there are other controls in place that restrict access to those systems, we check those and assess the risk rather than break anything. By the way, we always leave things as we found them, and document everything we did.

From a people perspective, not only do we assess your cybersecurity training, but we can also run our own phishing campaigns to get an idea for the effectiveness of that training. Funny example here, we were working with a client in SOUTH Korea. We ran a campaign that resembled their own HR website to entice their folks to click on links to enter a raffle for a free holiday. We littered this with spelling mistakes and even referenced head office in NORTH Korea. Approximately 50% of staff clicked the link, so immediately we could see that staff training should be a priority!

We have a ton of other tools we can deploy as you can imagine, but from experience we find that risk management, policies, processes and procedures are a real area of weakness for most clients, along with backups, disaster recovery, and incident response procedures.

Risk Assessment

Risk management is the systematic process of identifying, assessing, and mitigating threats or uncertainties that can affect your organization. It involves analyzing risks' likelihood and impact, developing strategies to minimize harm, and monitoring measures' effectiveness.

Probably the most well-known risk management framework is NIST RMF (Risk Management Framework). In the words of nist.gov themselves; "The NIST Risk Management Framework (RMF) provides a comprehensive, flexible, repeatable, and measurable 7-step process that any organization can use to manage information security and privacy risk for organizations and systems and links to a suite of NIST standards and guidelines to support implementation of risk management programs to meet the requirements of the Federal Information Security Modernization Act (FISMA). Managing organizational risk is paramount to effective information security and privacy programs; the RMF approach can be applied to new and legacy systems, any type of system or technology (e.g., IoT, control systems), and within any type of organization regardless of size or sector."

The definition of risk boils down to something like "the possibility of suffering harm or loss". Risks are not all bad either, the risk of hurricanes might be a good thing if you're in the storm shutter business. Clearly not all risks are created equal, good or bad, so we score each risk using the following formula:

Likelihood X Impact = Risk Score.

There are grids online where you can use these score to score the severity of your risks, but essentially you probably want to deal with your critical and high risks first. All of this of course aligns with your organizational appetite for risk (probably a statement from key stakeholders, airlines for example state that safety is their primary concern, meaning their risk tolerance is extremely low).

By the way there are different ways to deal with risks. For positive risks you might want to share or enhance those. But typically, risks are seen in a negative light, and treatments include accept, avoid, transfer or mitigate.

By the way, if you don't have one already, we can set you up with a risk register which is a central place for you to identify, categorize, assess and rate risks, track your response and assign an overall owner. We see risk management as a project or program of activities, so treating it as such with the register as your dashboard is a really useful way to proceed.

There are many different categories of risks, so classification is always useful: operational; reputational; competitive, technology; political – it all depends on you and your operating context, and the categories most relevant to you. Clearly our focus is on physical and cybersecurity, so we use our findings from both assessments to start to populate your risk register. Probably more importantly to you, we also suggest remediation strategies for all of our findings.

Chapter 2 - Physical Security Measures

Technology and Physical Security

Without wanting to start on a negative note, it's difficult to know where to start with this topic, because this area has seen a massive amount of innovation and change recently. Even traditional security solutions such as cameras and access control have seen significant changes and improvements. I did try to categorize the different technologies to make life easier, but gave up because many span multiple categories, and this is all interrelated now. So, below please find a list of technologies, split between 'non-crunchy' and 'crunchy', and in some kind of order of significance. Do please park in the back of your mind the new world of physical security technology in this chapter now incorporates many 'hooks' into the world of cybersecurity - call it Convergence, Chapter 4.

I like to keep things simple as you can probably tell by now. In my mind I see two sides to the topic of physical security technology – the hardware and data (crunchy bits) and the intelligence (non-crunchy bits). Let's start with the intelligence:

Non-Crunchy Technology

No prizes for guessing first up are Artificial Intelligence (AI) and Machine Learning (ML). This is the technology that is now the 'glue' to many complicated business processes and applications, and physical security is no exception. As we know, AI is fantastic at analyzing massive sets of data, and finding patterns. Imagine bringing all your live camera feed and LiDAR (Light Detection and Ranging – this will be in the crunchy bits section) data into one place and having AI figure out potential threats, predict incidents before they occur (that's more the ML piece – behavioral analysis). What impact would this have on public safety, especially schools, sporting events, military bases, entire cities?

Next up, digital twins. These are digital representations of physical objects (think about what console games look like where you navigate the landscape, and you get the picture). Digital twins allow your security teams to monitor physical locations (buildings, campuses, critical infrastructure) in real-time by creating a virtual version that replicates the actual environment. You feed in your camera data and any other sensors, and this enables a more interactive way of managing security, where teams can predict and respond to threats more efficiently. You can run simulations to identify weaknesses, but possibly more importantly to train your people what to do in the event of an emergency. You can also easily train the emergency services across all scenarios (including active shooters) using your actual building context. Augmented Reality (AR) is already being used in this context - AR glasses can overlay virtual threats on real-world environments, helping guards to practice handling dangerous situations in a controlled setting.

Now imagine if you were to combine AI and digital twins? Digital twins create a dynamic environment where changes in the physical world are mirrored in real-time in the digital version. This means potential threats can be detected, assessed, and mitigated more efficiently, making responses more proactive rather than reactive. We see a future where deaths of children by active shooters in schools is significantly reduced. As mentioned, that's why I started TSG.

This section wouldn't be complete without saying a few words about blockchain. I'll assume most of us know what this is and how it works, but ignoring its use in cryptocurrencies for now, in the context of physical security tamper-proof blockchain technology is being trialed for identity management and secure access. By decentralizing identity verification, blockchain can enhance security by ensuring that individual access credentials are tamper-proof and harder to hack. Blockchain is also incredibly useful for ensuring the integrity of data collected by physical security systems. Whether it's video footage, access logs, or sensor data, storing this information on a blockchain almost guarantees that the data is immutable and has not been tampered with. I say 'almost', because blockchain has been hacked. A quick search of the Web will tell you about that.

It's a little early to discuss quantum cryptography here, that's in 'The Future' chapter later in the book, but rest assured both the good and bad of quantum compute will be hitting our news feeds in the near future.

As we progress with the rest of this chapter, think about the impact of adding the crunchy technologies we are about to talk about to this AI-enabled digital twin.

Crunchy Technology

As mentioned, this is the 'hardware/data' side of the equation, but really these are the bits and pieces, including sensors and other technologies, that deliver relevant data to the non-crunchy bits to derive some form of intelligence, even insight.

Let's start with cameras. The digital camera revolution has been nothing short of amazing, with digital zoom and fantastic resolution, enabling clarity at much further distances. ML enhances surveillance systems by helping them interpret vast amounts of data more effectively. Traditional CCTV systems require human monitoring, but AI and ML-driven solutions can automatically flag suspicious activities and even control pan-tilt-zoom (PTZ) cameras to focus on areas of interest. This reduces the burden on human operators and almost ensures that nothing important is missed. In large urban areas, these systems are capable of managing multiple feeds simultaneously, identifying patterns of crime or identifying specific individuals of interest. ML systems can also learn from past data to predict crime hotspots or respond more quickly to developing incidents. Thermal cameras are increasingly being used to detect people or animals, even in complete darkness. Infrared imaging can also be applied to secure perimeters in remote or high-risk locations. We can include ALPR (Automatic License Plate Recognition) and container/aircraft recognition cameras either here or in the non-crunchy section.

Let's continue with LiDAR (Light Detection and Ranging), because combined with cameras and AI the world of perimeter security and has never looked so good. LiDAR technology uses lasers to create highly detailed 3D maps of environments, and is gaining traction in physical security due to its precision and range. Its applications include:

- Perimeter security: LiDAR can detect intruders by mapping the environment and identifying any changes, even in poor visibility conditions.

- Intrusion detection: LiDAR systems can accurately detect objects or people in real-time, distinguishing between animals, vehicles, and humans, which helps reduce false alarms.

- Crowd management: LiDAR can monitor and manage large crowds, analyzing density and movement to detect abnormal behavior in public spaces.

- Automated access control: LiDAR can be integrated with AI to manage secure access by analyzing the 3D profile of individuals or vehicles entering restricted areas.

Because of its high accuracy, range, and ability to work in any lighting conditions, LiDAR is increasingly favored for monitoring vast or outdoor critical infrastructure applications such airports, military bases, and smart cities.

Loosely related to LiDAR let's talk about Millimeter Wave (mmWave) technology. Both LiDAR and mmWave are revolutionizing detection and surveillance by offering more robust, real-time insights into physical security environments, providing enhanced situational awareness in high-risk or high-traffic areas. mmWave's two major applications are high-frequency wireless communication, and detection and imaging. mmWave scanners are widely used at airports and secure facilities (and we would like to see these at schools) to detect hidden weapons or contraband on individuals without physical contact. They work by emitting electromagnetic waves that reflect off objects, generating detailed images. mmWave can also detect movement and objects through walls or other barriers, making it valuable in law enforcement, search-and-rescue operations, and critical infrastructure monitoring. And unlike traditional cameras, mmWave is not affected by poor lighting or fog, and it is useful for monitoring areas where visual surveillance may be limited. We like mmWave because it can be used to count people without identifying them. We can't install cameras in restrooms, but in the event of a shooter emergency you'd want to know how many people were hiding in restrooms without contravening their data privacy rights - this is where mmWave comes in.

Next, the Internet of Things (IoT) in Security. This is the area that has seen arguably the most innovation – visit CES any time soon in Las Vegas and you'll see what I mean. The Internet of Things (IoT) has become a transformative force in the field of physical security, enabling systems to be more interconnected, intelligent, and responsive. By integrating a wide range of devices - sensors, cameras, alarms, and locks - into a unified network, IoT is enhancing the efficiency and effectiveness of security operations including detecting emergencies (e.g., fire, break-ins, or hazardous material spills) and automatically initiating response protocols. I could write a whole other book on just this topic, but sticking to the 'crunchy bits' topic the world of IoT in Security now offers gunshot detection, vape/drug detection, wearables (access control), digital signage, help (spoken keyword), panic buttons, sound levels (aggression), light levels, air quality levels.

The world of biometrics fits in around here. This world has moved a long way from simple fingerprint recognition. Now available are facial recognition, iris and retina scanning, palm vein and voice recognition, and a combination of any of those into multimodal biometrics solutions which fit into the world of multi-factor authentication (MFA). In the very near future Mr. Musk has plans around implanted technology, but personally I'd want to understand the levels of protection before I hook my body into a wider system.

I'll veer into the world of 'large and crunchy' for a second – security robots and drones. Both can and are being used for surveilling large areas (warehouses, even borders), and also crowd control. In some states you might be able to arm drones and use them against shooters, or if not wouldn't you rather a shooter be dispensing brass into something made of plastic and metal than human flesh? I believe Texas has approved the use of armed drones in certain situations. You have to love Texas.

While I'm here, and we'll get into this when we cover use cases for smart bases later in the book, let's mention sonar (fixed and portable). Ports are a critical component of any country's supply chain, and are most definitely classified as critical infrastructure, as are offshore oil rigs and dams. We are seeing sub-surface applications to detect submerged threats, detect and track divers and submarines or anyone approaching sensitive locations. We have even been asked to assist a port (in a country you wouldn't necessarily visit for a vacation) to detect covert packages being attached to legitimate cargo vessels in the fight against international drug trafficking.

Back to more basic 'crunchy' technology, we see advances in smart glass technology to enable windows to transition from clear to opaque at the press of a button, helping to prevent visual access to secure areas. Also, new bulletproof materials (e.g., lightweight composites) are being integrated into both building designs and personal protective equipment (PPE) to enhance physical resilience. Bulletproof backpacks for schools? Yes, they are now a thing. Sadly.

At the end of the day, when it comes to critical infrastructure the first step is always the physical security of people and systems. Unauthorized access must be prevented to avoid sabotage. There should be physical access controls in place such as key cards, biometrics, and video surveillance to protect OT and IT assets from unauthorized physical access. We have to ensure OT control rooms and key infrastructure are hardened and only accessible to trained personnel.

Which brings us to the next chapter, cybersecurity for critical infrastructure.

Chapter 3 - Cybersecurity for Critical Infrastructure

Another massive topic. What we're looking at here isn't just securing all the data generated by the crunchy bits noted earlier to ensure its integrity, but the wider data essential for running and maintaining businesses, bases, schools, cities – and the citizens so intrinsically linked to all of this. So, company data, intellectual property and secrets, personally identifiable information (PII) such as social security and national insurance numbers, addresses and driver's licenses, passports, credit cards – the list is almost endless. Do think about how the world is evolving when it comes to data – smart cities have to be supported by huge data lakes (distributed or not) or they just will not be able to function. The point is, the value of data as a commodity is often overlooked. Fact is, we should all pay a lot more attention to how we protect it, what we share, and what people do with it. There's a personal element that I can't emphasize enough – we all need to do better – especially with our own data.

I won't go into WHY bad actors want to either mess with your access to, change, or steal your data, that's for another book, just know it's a huge problem and the attack surface (the bits that bad actors find vulnerabilities in) is growing by the day. And as we merge our data in databases or data lakes to make our smart city lives more convenient, the value of the data increases so the bad guys will try even harder to get at it. Even when our data is in many different places (local laptop, company server, cloud, different country), because of the way it is all being linked to make it useful, a breach in one place can mean all your data across those locations could be compromised.

Now in the context of critical infrastructure, the ramifications of a cybersecurity breach could be catastrophic. In the introduction I listed some examples, so I won't labor that point here (nuclear winter anyone?), but think about smart cities and their components – what if someone compromised the traffic lights system, or water purification for a city, or garbage collection, or stole the personal data of all the residents of a city....the impact is always felt by the citizens, so I feel the citizens should have a say in how their data is protected, and frankly also bear much more personal responsibility in who is allowed access to their data in the first place. As we often say in our business, people are our first line of defense, but also our weakest link. So, let's start there.

Educating People on Cyber Safety

You don't have to try too hard to find statistics on the Internet for people and companies being swindled out of information or money by clicking the wrong link or responding to an email. I believe we all know the Nigerian Prince who wants to send you millions of dollars if you just give him your bank details is a scam. Problem is, the intent of these scams is the same, but the sophistication of their delivery has grown exponentially, and is getting worse as bad actors use AI. It used to be just badly worded phishing emails, and texts, then voice simulation, and now video deepfakes. Recently a company in Hong Kong was separated from $25M of its hard-earned revenue because the CFO was convinced on a Zoom call to send the money by a video deepfake of the CEO. We're all under attack on a daily basis. But there are some things we can do to reduce our risk. Here are a few simple examples:

- Recognize and Avoid Phishing Scams - hover over links before clicking, look for red flags like urgent language, misspellings, or unfamiliar senders, and never provide sensitive information via email or text unless you can verify the sender's authenticity.

- Multi-Factor Authentication (MFA) – one of the most effective way to secure your accounts, in fact most banks now insist you set this up (because they were losing so much money to scammers!). Authenticator applications are also really useful, but even a plain old text for verification is better than nothing.
- The Importance of Strong, Unique Passwords – if you use just one, weak password for everything because it's easy to remember, well, my mum used to say a fool and their money are easily separated. Use a password manager which can even generate and save passwords for you. And makes it easy to have unique passwords. Add MFA to the mix and you have a winning combination.
- Back Up Your Data Regularly – if you are the victim of a ransomware attack, this is how we get you up and running quickly without paying a ransom.
- And a bucket of random but good advice – recognize the threats of using public Wi-Fi and social engineering, use a VPN when in public, verify requests for information, and don't download untrusted software.

Protecting Operational Technology (OT)

Protecting Operational Technology (OT) is crucial because OT systems, which control physical processes in the critical infrastructure sector, are increasingly becoming targets for cyber-attacks. Historically, OT systems were isolated (you might hear the term 'air gapped', which means not connected to other networks), but with the rise of Industry 4.0 (that's another book, have a Google), they are now connected to IT networks, making them vulnerable to cyber threats. Add the legacy nature of these systems and their inherent lack of security, and you have a recipe for disaster. Add IoT and IIoT if you want a cherry on your cake. Hackers want to use these weak systems to gain access to your wider network, or cause disruption by breaking systems and data flows.

Fear not, there are ways to reduce the exposure and the risk – here are some effective strategies below. By the way, a lot of people think "cybersecurity" is all about funky new AI technology to prevent hacks. Well yes, it is, but it's also about governance, risk, compliance, people and process, which is why the funky AI protection is not first in the list below (first is always people awareness training, but that's above):

- Segmentation of IT and OT Networks. This is a network architecture solution. We didn't have a problem when these systems were isolated, so let's isolate them as much as we can without breaking them. This means putting them on a separate OT network with firewalls and only allowing the connectivity they need to the wider IT network to be able to function. We reduce the attack surface and the ability of an attacker to move laterally (that's what they want to do – move from OT into your Finance systems!)
- Implement Strong Access Control – also known as Role Based Access Control (RBAC). This is a process solution. Give your people access to ONLY those systems and data that they need to be able to do their jobs, and restrict the rest of it. Also known as the principle of least privilege. Bonus tip – pay special attention to third-party vendors who might need temporary access for maintenance. That fish tank in Vegas? Third party maintenance company breach.
- Regular Patching and Vulnerability Management. Another boring process solution, but OT systems (and IT systems for that matter) often run legacy software, which may be vulnerable to known exploits. Regular patching is essential to close security gaps. Hackers know about the vulnerabilities and how to exploit them, so in the example of a remote access vulnerability (these are critical for obvious reasons) all they need is

to find a system that has not been patched and in they come.
- Continuous Monitoring and Threat Detection. At last, a funky technology solution! AI is fabulous for finding trends in data. Which makes it great for monitoring the different behaviors on your network (file, system, network, endpoint) and reacting as you wish depending on what it finds. Anti-virus is almost a thing of the past, the market is deep into XDR (eXtended Detection and Response). Add to this intrusion detection systems (IDS), intrusion prevention systems (IPS), and security information and event management (SIEM) systems specifically tailored for OT environments and your risk of breach is very low indeed (if configured correctly and patched when needed). Network traffic encryption would take this to the next level.
- Comprehensive Risk Assessments. Another process solution, but many governance frameworks insist on this happening annually. Please refer to Chapter 1 for all the details, but in the case of critical infrastructure we'd look at OT-specific risk assessments, taking into account the potential operational impacts of both physical and cyber threats. Use tools like NIST SP 800-82 or IEC 62443 frameworks to assess risks, and prioritize securing critical OT assets.
- Incident Response and Recovery Planning. Here we suggest having and regularly testing an Incident Response Plan for IT and OT environments. Develop and regularly test OT-specific incident response playbooks that cover common scenarios like ransomware, DDoS attacks, or insider threats. Create backup and recovery procedures that are regularly updated and stored offline to ensure critical systems can be restored quickly in the event of an attack. Retain an expert third-party company as extra insurance. Did I tell you the story about how we fixed a hacked major global sporting event? Message me for details.

There are other solutions and principles you'd want to look at, like the principle of Zero Trust and definitely securing any remote access you have enabled to your systems. If there's more you want to know or have questions on any of this, you are welcome to reach to me and anyone in my team at Stealth-ISS Group or Total Security Global and we'll be happy to chat with you. This book was never intended to be exhaustive, although I do hope you use it as a high-level reference manual if you need it.

Where we'd like the world to be, and especially the US, is for organizations handling critical infrastructure, for all of the above security strategies to OT security to be viewed as non-negotiable due to the potential consequences of successful cyber-attacks. These best practices, when properly implemented, can help to significantly reduce risks in OT environments, ensuring that the availability, integrity, and safety of industrial control systems (ICS) are maintained. Meaning our critical infrastructure which runs on OT and ICS cannot be compromised.

Cloud Security

The best definition I've heard of 'cloud compute' is "somebody else's datacenter". Major companies have saved a ton of money over time by outsourcing datacenter services to third parties who have become specialists in that business. I should know, I used to be part of that world. Sounds great, right?

The problems, from experience and observation having been one of those outsourcers and an auditor of cloud companies, is that the cloud folks have had a tendency to oversell their security services, and the outsourcer has felt (or been led to believe) they could take much less responsibility, and accountability, for their data. In the middle lies much of your risk. (These are personal observations, nothing to do with any of my companies, and no names have been used at the request of our lawyers.)

It's at this point in the book you should be starting to see some recurring themes when it comes to protecting your data, be that locally or in the cloud. This is because they are GREAT things to do! So, you should notice the size of the chapters get shorter as I refer you back to things above.

Anyway, that risk in the middle piece I mentioned above – here are some ways to reduce that risk:

- Review your cloud contract and check what you are paying for when it comes to security of your data. Then get an expert opinion on whether that's good enough, and if not, get a list of things you might need. Then, talk to your cloud provider to a) check what you've paid for is actually in place, and b) get a price for the things the expert said you should have, and figure out the risk/reward of paying for those, or not.
- Find a way to encrypt your data at rest. Your data is in someone else's building (who knows how many or in what country, and that can be important when dealing with the federal government), so you will want to make it unintelligible to anyone from that company who might have access to it as part of their support function. And anyone else for that matter.
- Find a way to encrypt your data in transit. The network links between your entity and the cloud provider – switch on encryption please. Critical infrastructure organizations should consider end-to-end encryption, ensuring only authorized entities can decrypt the data, even if the cloud provider is compromised.
- Multi-Factor Authentication. See above.
- Zero trust Security Framework. This one means different things to different people, and we'd be happy to get into detail with you on what this means to you, but in essence we assume no one - internal or external

– is trusted by default. Only authorized users can access specific parts of the infrastructure. It's a mix of segmentation, RBAC, continuous validation and dynamic policies including user behavior and location. Too much to get into here, but happy to help.
- Cloud Security Posture Management (CSPM). This is really cool and involves a scan of cloud environments for misconfigured storage, excessive permissions, or unprotected services. You're checking that what you've paid for is in place, all of the time. Cloud providers have been known to make changes....
- Privileged Access Management (PAM). Use PAM solutions to manage and monitor privileged accounts. Implement role-based access control (RBAC) to minimize who has access to critical systems. Privileged users should be regularly reviewed and have their activities logged and audited. It's the privileged accounts the hackers want to control, because they are the keys to your data and systems kingdom.
- Other things we've already mentioned – regular assessments and regulatory compliance, continuous monitoring and threat detection, security automation and incident response.
- One last point on cloud – data sovereignty. I mentioned these cloud providers are global, and your data could literally be anywhere. Well, know where your data resides and ensure it complies with data sovereignty laws. Different countries have varying data protection laws that may restrict where critical infrastructure data can be stored. Ensure that your cloud provider offers data centers in regions that comply with your jurisdiction's data sovereignty requirements. If needed, implement geo-fencing to ensure data stays within legal borders.

IoT and IIoT

There's no getting away from it, IoT and IIoT (Industrial Internet of Things) are here to stay. Mainly for reasons of cost, convenience, rapid innovation, and many more. The problem is they are inherently insecure

Securing IoT (Internet of Things) and IIoT (Industrial Internet of Things) in the context of critical infrastructure is a complex challenge due to the increasing connectivity of physical systems with digital networks. IoT/IIoT devices are often deployed in critical environments like energy grids, water treatment plants, manufacturing, and transportation systems, making them prime targets for cyber-attacks. These devices often lack built-in security features and are deployed in environments where system uptime is critical, adding complexity to securing them. Back in the day, the first IoT devices used a chipset that had literally no room on it to store any sort of security functionality! Those devices are still out there. Weakest link and all that.

Securing IoT and IIoT devices in critical infrastructure is not just about implementing individual security tools but also about adopting a holistic, multi-layered approach. By considering the unique challenges of OT environments, such as operational uptime and device lifecycle management, and combining cybersecurity best practices with physical protections, we have to create a secure environment that mitigates the risks posed by increasingly interconnected devices. Here are some ideas to reduce your risk:

- Device Authentication. Each IoT/IIoT device should have a unique identity and robust authentication mechanisms to ensure that only authorized devices can connect to the network. Implement strong, mutual authentication protocols (such as X.509 certificates or digital signatures) for device communication. Use Public Key Infrastructure (PKI) to securely manage device identities and enforce strict authentication protocols for any device joining the network.

- Physical Security of IoT/IIoT Devices. Deploy physical security measures such as tamper-resistant enclosures, surveillance, and access controls for critical IoT/IIoT devices. Consider implementing hardware security modules (HSMs) or trusted platform modules (TPMs) that can store cryptographic keys securely on devices.
- Share any threat intelligence with other critical infrastructure entities to build a shared defense. Join industry-specific Information Sharing and Analysis Centers (ISACs) to share threat intelligence and best practices. Leverage threat intelligence feeds to stay up to date on the latest IoT/IIoT threats and vulnerabilities, and integrate these feeds into security operations. Or find an expert to do this for you.
- These are the only three new suggestions I have, but here's a list of measures already covered that you might want to revisit:
    - Network segmentation
    - Zero Trust Architecture
    - Endpoint Protection (XDR)
    - Patching – software, firmware, etc. Vulnerability management
    - Encrypt data at rest and in transit
    - Secure all remote access
    - Intrusion detection system (IDS)
    - Backup your data
    - Have a tested Incident Response Plan

Responding to Cyber Threats and Incidents - IRP

We've talked in this book about the different types of cyber threats, and quite honestly if I put detailed words to paper about that here the cyber threat landscape will likely have changed by the time this book is published. Needless to say, the bad guys want to keep you from your data, steal your data, or change it for their benefit. How they do that changes over time.

We could all spend a fortune on cyber defenses, but it takes just one poorly configured server, or one click of a link in an email, and all of a sudden, we have an incident on our hands. This is why we believe (and so do many governance frameworks) that everyone should have an Incident Response Plan, that is tested (tabletop exercises) regularly. From experience we know that the quicker an incident is responded to and contained, the quicker you can regain operations. Let alone the significantly reduced cost (money and reputation) of doing this.

There are 7 main elements to an Incident Response Plan (IRP), in fact you could almost call it 7 plans in an incident response program. This is important so I'll get into the weeds a bit here.

1. Preparation. The preparation phase is the foundation of an effective IRP and ensures that the organization is ready to respond to an incident swiftly and effectively. The focus is on building a capable incident response team, creating playbooks, and ensuring proper tools are in place.

1.1 Incident Response Team (IRT)

- Composition: The IRT typically includes members from IT, security, legal, communications, and HR. For larger organizations, this might also involve business unit leaders, external consultants, or even law enforcement.
- Training: All members must undergo regular training and simulations to ensure they are familiar with their roles. Tabletop exercises help prepare for different scenarios, from ransomware to data breaches.
- Tools: The team should have access to the right tools, such as endpoint detection and response (EDR)

systems, intrusion detection systems (IDS), and forensic tools.

1.2 Asset Inventory and Risk Assessment

- Asset Identification: Document all critical assets, including systems, applications, and data. This helps prioritize what must be protected and recovered first during an incident.
- Risk Analysis: Identify potential risks and vulnerabilities specific to the organization's assets, and determine which threats are most likely to affect them (e.g., ransomware, insider threats, supply chain attacks).

2. Identification - The goal of the identification phase is to detect security incidents as early as possible to minimize damage. This requires constant monitoring and advanced detection mechanisms to quickly assess whether an incident has occurred and its potential scope. We've covered these but worth re-iterating for the sake of completeness of this section

2.1 Incident Detection

- Monitoring: Use Security Information and Event Management (SIEM) systems to collect, aggregate, and analyze data from logs, network traffic, and endpoints. Anomaly detection systems powered by AI or machine learning can flag deviations from normal activity.
- Incident Indicators: Common indicators of compromise (IoCs) include abnormal user behavior, sudden spikes in network traffic, unauthorized access attempts, malware signatures, or unusual data exfiltration activities.

2.2 Incident Classification

- Severity Levels: Define clear categories for incidents based on their potential impact on the organization. For example, a phishing email may be classified as a low-priority event, while a ransomware infection encrypting critical systems is high priority.
- Immediate Actions: Depending on the classification, initial response actions can range from simply observing the activity to immediately shutting down affected systems to prevent further damage.

3. Containment - Containment involves taking immediate steps to limit the scope and impact of an incident, once it is clear that you are, indeed, in an incident. The goal is to stop the attack from spreading while ensuring that systems are maintained or recovered with minimal disruption.

3.1 Short-Term Containment

- Isolation: Disconnect infected systems or devices from the network. This could mean severing specific devices or subnets to stop the lateral movement of the attack. (Note, you may be asked to keep the infected node on the network to learn more about the attack.)
- Backup Segregation: Ensure that backups are isolated from infected systems. Attackers, especially in ransomware cases, very often try to encrypt or delete backups to strengthen their position in pressuring organizations into paying the ransom.
- If this is ransomware and it cannot be contained or quickly remediated, you may find yourself having to negotiate with the threat actor for a rapid resolution. Can we suggest you hire a professional to do this, with an experienced Incident Commander, in full view of your Legal and communications people. This piece is worthy of its own chapter, but do reach out if this is something you need more detail on.

3.2 Long-Term Containment

- Patching Vulnerabilities: For long-term containment, address the vulnerabilities or misconfigurations that led to the breach. This might include applying patches, tightening access controls, or changing compromised credentials.
- Network Segmentation: Implementing or adjusting network segmentation can help contain an attack by limiting access between different areas of the network.

4. Eradication - The eradication phase focuses on removing the threat entirely from the network. This can involve malware removal, vulnerability fixes, or clearing compromised accounts.

4.1 Malware Removal

- Tools: Use antivirus or antimalware solutions to remove malicious software from affected systems. In some cases, manual intervention may be required to identify deeply embedded malware or rootkits.
- Endpoint Scans: Conduct comprehensive scans of all systems to ensure there are no residual traces of malware or unauthorized access points.

4.2 Patching and Hardening

- Vulnerability Patching: Identify the vulnerabilities that were exploited and patch them across all systems. This could involve applying software updates or firmware patches.
- System Hardening: Implement stronger security controls, such as enforcing multi-factor authentication (MFA), disabling unused services, and adjusting firewall rules to strengthen security.

5. Recovery - In the recovery phase, the focus is on restoring affected systems and services to normal operation while ensuring the incident has been fully resolved.

5.1 Restoring Systems

- Data Restoration: Use clean backups to restore affected systems to a pre-incident state. Verify the integrity of the restored data and systems to ensure they have not been compromised.
- Testing: Before bringing systems back online, perform thorough testing to ensure that they are functioning correctly and free of threats.

5.2 Monitoring Post-Incident

- Enhanced Monitoring: Continue to monitor the environment closely to detect any signs of residual malware or follow-up attacks. This is particularly important in targeted attacks where attackers may attempt to regain access.

6. Post-Incident Review - After the incident has been resolved, conducting a post-incident review is critical for identifying lessons learned, areas for improvement, and any systemic issues that need addressing.

6.1 Root Cause Analysis

- Forensic Investigation: Conduct a detailed forensic investigation to understand how the attack occurred, which vulnerabilities were exploited, and what the attackers' goals were. This includes examining logs, network traffic, and affected systems.
- Threat Actor Analysis: If applicable, identify the threat actor group responsible for the attack. This can help organizations understand their adversary's tactics and prepare for similar attacks in the future.

6.2 Lessons Learned

- Team Review: Conduct a review meeting with the incident response team to identify what worked well and where improvements are needed. Evaluate the efficiency of detection, containment, communication, and eradication efforts.
- Incident Report: Document the incident in a formal report that outlines the timeline of events, actions taken, and the final resolution. Share this with key stakeholders to maintain transparency and accountability.

7. Continuous Improvement and Policy Updates - After an incident, it's essential to refine processes and update policies to better defend against future threats.

7.1 Update Security Controls

- Strengthening Defenses: Based on lessons learned, implement new controls to reduce the risk of future incidents. This may involve tightening firewall policies, implementing role-based access control (RBAC), or upgrading outdated software.
- Refining Detection Capabilities: Update SIEM rules, IDS signatures, and logging policies to improve threat detection based on attack vectors observed during the incident.

7.2 Training and Awareness

- Employee Training: Conduct additional training for staff to improve awareness of security threats. For example, if the attack was initiated by a phishing email, train employees on how to recognize and report phishing attempts.
- Incident Response Simulations: Perform regular tabletop exercises or red team/blue team simulations to test the incident response plan and improve the team's readiness for future incidents.

AI and Cybersecurity

The section you've all been waiting for, right? Well, if you wanted the low-down from an industry veteran, my wife, Dasha Davies, has recently written a book which is available on Amazon called " Beyond Binary: AI and Cybersecurity: A Journey through Innovation, Risk and Ethical Consideration for a Secure Tomorrow", ISBN: B0D4LYH4ZH. I'm sure I can get you a free electronic copy if you reach out to me.

Anyway, what I will do here though is give my 60,000 feet opinion. Safe to say, we've seen a big difference in the volume and complexity of cyber-attacks since the bad guys were able to get their hands on AI and have it write and check their code for them. They have been able to industrialize their nefarious operations. This means phishing attacks actually look good and no longer have poor grammar, deepfakes are on the rise as mentioned, and it's just more difficult to spot the bad stuff.

Fear not though, AI has ridden to the rescue. The world of cyber protection has had to pivot away from signature-based software into taking more of a behavior-based approach. Remember I said AI is great and seeing patterns in vast swathes of data? Well, if that data all pertains to the distinct and unique behaviors of your organization, then AI can spot when some malware is causing something in your company to act in a way that it otherwise would not. It can then go investigate, and ML can (once learned) make do something about it.

Let me give you an example. XDR software continuously checks the behavior of your enterprise looking at endpoints, files, the network and user behavior. If some malware managed to evade your protections, settled down, and was trying to slowly exfiltrate data to a host in say, China, at 2AM on a Sunday, even if it were just a few bytes, the XDR would see that as an anomaly and alert you, the human, to investigate.

In more extreme and obvious cases, such as your endpoints being taken over to contribute to some global DDoS attack, you would have playbooks configured to spot that and take the node off the network immediately. In some cases, you'd want to quarantine the node and check it, and in others you'd want to completely reboot and format the node removing everything on it (uncommon as typically you'd want to forensically investigate the node and malware).

AI is not a panacea or silver bullet for cyber-attacks, but it sure beats having nothing. For AI to be truly effective, it must be continuously fine-tuned because of the rapidly evolving threat landscape, aligned with human oversight, and deployed with careful consideration of its limitations. As the digital and physical worlds continue to converge in critical infrastructure, AI's role in securing these environments will only become more essential.

Considerations for AI

I would be remiss if I didn't say a few words about what we as humans need to know and do when it comes to AI. I'm going to use the lovely consulting word salad of 'paradigm shift', because for once that phrase is completely relevant. AI is changing the game, and there is much to consider from the human perspective. Things to think about, especially if you are responsible for OT, smart city security, anything senior in critical infrastructure:

- Don't assume the answer that AI gives you is correct. Even GPT will warn you of this. A human being is required, complete with gut feel in some cases, to validate.

- Secure your AI – are your humans interacting with AI and asking it to do what you want it to do? This is a great opportunity to think about a boring old company policy – think of a policy as guardrails for your humans.
- In a similar vein, did you know that the data you input to AI becomes part of the wider data set? This means it ostensibly becomes public. Are you inadvertently sharing your sensitive data with your competitors or threat actors?
- If you expect the use of AI to materialize staffing savings and other efficiencies, what will you do with those displaced humans? Can I suggest before you return them to industry, that you train them to be your AI operators?
- Algorithmic bias and ethical considerations – imagine the large language model (LLM) you have chosen to use for your AI project was built by, say, Ford. And imagine your project is to design the vehicle of the future. Given the Ford LLM model was likely fed a load of Ford-specific data, what are the chances your new project car will look a lot like a Ford? Now that might be an unlikely scenario specific to cars, but do we believe governments and foreign adversaries would be above trying to sway population decisions in any way possible?

Without going all Terminator 2 and Skynet on you, let's practice some forward thinking and deploy some guardrails on AI before it goes sentient and sees humans as its biggest threat. A well-known social media company did observe two of its robots (Bob and Alice) invented their own language so their communication could be more efficient. Ultimately, shouldn't a human be the ultimate decision makes and have the ability to 'switch it off'?

Chapter 4 - Cyber-Physical Convergence

I hope you agree it makes sense at this point to talk about the convergence of cyber and physical security, just because delivering one separately from the other in the real-world would be more expensive. And less effective. But, also more complicated, it increases the attack surface, and therefore could be seen to be increasing your risk?

What is it?

Well, it's kind-of obvious from the title but there's a lot to it as you'll see. Cyber-Physical Convergence is the integration of physical security systems with digital networks and cybersecurity, leading to a seamless blend where both the physical and cyber domains are interconnected. This convergence allows for enhanced situational awareness, automated responses, and unified threat detection across both types of systems. In the modern era, where digital transformation is rapidly accelerating, the convergence of these two domains is increasingly essential for comprehensive security. Unless there's a clear mandate or conflict of interest for not doing so – casinos would be an example of this. That said, it's not all roses:

Key Considerations – The Downside

Physical Systems at Risk from Cyber Attacks.
Cyber-physical convergence means that traditionally physical security systems - such as surveillance cameras, building management systems, or industrial control systems (ICS) - are now at risk from cyber-attacks. If these systems are connected to the Internet, they can potentially be hacked to disable physical security measures:

- Disabling Alarms or Cameras: Hackers can exploit vulnerabilities in digital security systems to disable cameras or alarms, allowing unauthorized physical access without detection.
- Manipulating Building Systems: Critical infrastructure, like smart buildings or power grids, could be attacked by hackers who manipulate control systems, creating physical hazards like temperature spikes or power outages.

Cyber-Physical Systems (CPS) in Critical Infrastructure

Critical infrastructure sectors such as energy, transportation, and manufacturing heavily depend on Cyber-Physical Systems (CPS). These systems integrate computational elements with physical processes, meaning any cyber incident could have direct physical consequences:

- Energy Grids: In power plants or smart grids, cyber-attacks on Industrial Control Systems (ICS) or Supervisory Control and Data Acquisition (SCADA) systems can result in physical disruptions, such as blackouts or equipment damage. Or worse.
- Smart Cities: In urban environments, cyber-attacks on smart transportation systems or building management systems could disrupt public transportation, traffic flow, or even public safety.

Converged Threats: Insider Risks.

The rise of insider threats is a major challenge in cyber-physical convergence. Insiders with access to both physical spaces and digital systems are uniquely positioned to cause harm:

- Cyber-Physical Attacks: An employee might gain unauthorized access to a secure physical area (such as a data center) and install malicious software on the company's network. This type of converged attack can bypass security measures in both domains if not monitored.

IoT/IIoT and Cybersecurity Risks.
As IoT devices (like security cameras, smart locks, and environmental sensors) become more widespread in physical security, they introduce cyber vulnerabilities as I mentioned earlier. These devices are often connected to the corporate network, and your OT network, which means they can be hacked if not properly secured. Attackers can use compromised devices to gain a foothold in the network, causing a cyber-physical attack. If this happens on your corporate network and it's not sufficiently separated from your OT network, then all of a sudden, the problem could become much more significant from a critical infrastructure perspective. Worse, if your IIoT devices are compromised they are already on the OT network. Same problem but quicker. This convergence forces security teams to think about both physical and cyber defenses when deploying IoT/IIoT devices:

- Threat Detection and Response: If an IoT device is compromised, a converged system can initiate actions in both domains. For example, an attack on a security camera might result in network isolation of that camera and increased physical monitoring in the area it covers.
- Network Segmentation: Critical IoT devices can (and I would argue should) be segmented into dedicated networks, reducing the risk of a compromise spreading from one device to others.

Key Considerations – What You Need to Do

Unified Security Monitoring and Control.
One of the key aspects of cyber-physical convergence is the ability to monitor and control both physical and digital systems from a single platform. We call this a 'single pane of glass' but it's also known as 'mission control' or 'command central'. You get the picture. Here's an example. Our security operations center (SOC) manages both physical access control systems (door locks,

surveillance cameras, LiDAR) and cyber defenses (firewalls, intrusion detection systems, XDR as discussed) through one unified interface. This allows our security team, with the help of AI (because this can be a lot of data), to correlate the data from physical sensors and digital logs, creating a holistic view of the threat landscape. AI gets us trend data and usually some insight as to what's happening. For instance, if a cyber-attack is detected on the client network, it might be linked to an unauthorized access attempt in a physical location, which can be identified through IoT-enabled surveillance cameras or access control logs. We get a wider view of what's going on, so our response might be better, quicker, etc.

Automation and Incident Response.
With cyber-physical convergence, automated responses become more sophisticated. For example, if a physical breach is detected (e.g., someone trying to force open a door), the system can automatically:
- Lockdown nearby doors, increasing physical security.
- Trigger cybersecurity measures, such as isolating affected networks or increasing surveillance of digital systems.
- Notify both physical and cybersecurity teams, ensuring a coordinated response.

The same is true from the other perspective: a cyber-attack can trigger physical security measures, such as locking down access points or securing server rooms, preventing physical tampering during a cyber breach.

Threat Detection with AI and ML.
The integration of Artificial Intelligence (AI) and Machine Learning (ML) into both physical and cyber domains amplifies threat detection. These systems analyze vast amounts of data from both physical devices (e.g., motion detectors, cameras) and cyber systems (e.g., network traffic logs, access patterns) to identify anomalies:

- Predictive Security: ML models can predict potential security incidents based on historical patterns. For instance, unusual access to both a physical area (e.g., a server room) and an online system (e.g., administrative credentials) at the same time might signal an insider threat or coordinated attack.
- Anomaly Detection: AI can flag behaviors that deviate from the norm, such as an employee accessing sensitive areas at odd hours, combined with abnormal network activity, suggesting a breach.

Zero Trust Security Models.

If it wasn't a pretty good idea already, the rise of cyber-physical convergence encourages the adoption of the Zero Trust Security Model, which assumes that threats could come from both internal and external actors, and no system or person should automatically be trusted. Zero Trust applies across the board:

- Network Access: Only authorized personnel and devices are granted access to both physical areas and network resources after thorough verification.
- Continuous Verification: Users and devices are continuously monitored for signs of compromise, even after access is initially granted.

Blockchain for Cyber-Physical Convergence.

Blockchain can play a role in cyber-physical convergence by ensuring that data integrity is maintained across both domains. By creating immutable records of physical access logs and cyber events, blockchain helps to ensure that both physical and digital security events are properly logged and cannot be tampered with:

- Distributed Ledger Technology (DLT) can provide a single source of truth for verifying physical access to facilities, as well as digital actions taken on a network. This is especially useful for auditing and compliance in highly regulated industries, and of course critical infrastructure.

Is it worth it?

Cyber-physical convergence represents the blending of physical and digital security systems, creating a more comprehensive approach to modern threats. It's another risk/reward decision for me. Convergence brings a lower cost, in my opinion, but you could argue an increased risk if you don't 'do it properly'. As both domains increasingly overlap, ensuring that they work together seamlessly will be critical for protecting critical infrastructure, organizations, and individuals from a new generation of complex, hybrid threats. So, my personal answer would be yes, the pearl is worth the dive, as long as you fully understand the downside and deliver the right tools and architecture accordingly. If you half-ass it, all you really did was increase the attack surface. Not a decision to be taken lightly.

Chapter 5 - People

At the start of the book, I mentioned I'd be working within the three pillars of People, Process, and Technology. And Governance, Risk and Compliance (which are more underlying themes and less pillars). Let's be honest though, this is predominantly a book about technology. And security. In the context of critical infrastructure of course.

I've mentioned People and Process fleetingly along the way, but before we conclude the book with how to design secure critical infrastructure and facilities, I felt it was appropriate to dig into People and Process a bit more. Because without these, technology alone is naked and afraid.

I said it before and I'll say it again, People are your first line of defense, but also your weakest link. Technology at its core is pretty simple – you tell it what to do, and it does that time and again. Even AI and ML – they are not sentient (yet) – they have to be instructed and taught by people. Technology for the most part is consistent and predictable. People can be the exact opposite.

We've discussed hackers, who may or not have a heartbeat, insider threats and even negligence and accidents which can negatively impact critical infrastructure operations. The hacker piece we mostly cover off with technology, so that's not included here. Below are some people-related considerations to reduce the risk that critical infrastructure carries when it comes to the people involved.

Background Checks

A crucial element of pre-employment screening, security assessments, and compliance in many industries, and tend to be mandatory when sensitive data or critical infrastructure is involved. Individuals working with sensitive information or managing critical systems need to be thoroughly vetted for both criminal activity and financial vulnerabilities, as these can increase the risk of malicious actions, such as sabotage or theft of proprietary data. Insider threat is real. In 2013 Ricky Joe Mitchell, a former employee of EnerVest Operating LLC, a major oil and gas company, after learning that he was about to be fired, retaliated by sabotaging the company's systems. He used his privileged access to the company's network to disable the company's backup systems. He also deleted important company files, which were essential for the company's ongoing operations. The sabotage caused significant disruption to the company's operations, and it took EnerVest over 30 days to recover fully from the damage. Mitchell was later sentenced to four years in prison for his actions, which EnerVest probably felt was not enough given the disruption he caused.

We don't know the extent of the checks made on Mitchell. We do know he did not have a criminal record, and for some checks that would be enough. However, on investigation, it was revealed that in 1996, when he was a high school student, he had confessed to implanting 108 computer viruses into the school's computer system.

What would have prevented this, or minimized the disruption? Technology! Role Based Access Control (RBAC), XDR (behavior monitoring), File Integrity Monitoring (FIM) to name but a few. And Process! - a tested Incident Response Plan would have saved time, along with maybe a decent data backup architecture/strategy.

This example shows that while background checks are crucial, they may not always capture behavioral issues from earlier stages of a person's life, especially if the incidents occurred during youth or did not result in formal charges or convictions. In this case, even though Mitchell had displayed early signs of risky behavior, it would not have shown up in a typical criminal background check. Hence, in critical infrastructure roles, it's also important to conduct behavioral assessments.

Behavioral assessment

Involves evaluating a candidate's or employee's psychological traits, decision-making processes, and personality characteristics that could pose security risks, especially in critical infrastructure settings. It focuses on qualities like trustworthiness, impulsiveness, reaction to stress, and moral judgment. Here are a few of the more well-known types with a few examples:

- Situational Judgment Tests (SJTs): Present individuals with hypothetical, work-related situations and ask them to choose the most appropriate response. This reveals how they might handle security incidents, ethical dilemmas, or emergencies.
- Emotional Intelligence (EI) Assessments: Focus on how well individuals can manage their own emotions and understand others'. People with high EI are typically better at conflict resolution and managing stressful environments, which is crucial for reducing insider threats.
- Psychometric Testing: Measures personality traits, cognitive ability, and behavioral tendencies. Tools like DISC assessments (Dominance, Influence, Steadiness, Compliance) can give insight into how individuals might respond to specific challenges in a security-focused role.
- Personality tests: Tools like the Big Five Personality Traits (openness, conscientiousness, extraversion, agreeableness, neuroticism) or Myers-Briggs Type Indicator can highlight behavioral tendencies that are important for certain security-related roles.

- Integrity tests, AKA Axiological tests: These tests evaluate an individual's ethical beliefs and their likelihood of engaging in dishonest or malicious behavior. Axiology is the branch of philosophy that deals with values, including both ethics (moral values) and aesthetics (values related to beauty). In the context of integrity tests, the focus is on moral values, particularly how individuals evaluate what is right and wrong, and how those evaluations guide their behavior. (We use these for our key hires, as do the FBI allegedly, for pre-poly testing.)
- Cognitive and emotional response tests: These focus on how well an individual can manage emotions, make decisions under pressure, and solve complex problems.

Do bear in mind, while these tests are useful, they are not infallible. Individuals might attempt to manipulate their answers to present themselves in a better light. Also, ethical standards can vary between cultures, meaning that what is considered unethical in one society might be more accepted in another. I've lived all over the world; I know this to be true. It's crucial that integrity tests are used as part of a broader hiring or employee evaluation process, alongside interviews, reference checks, and continuous monitoring – see below.

Assuming you've performed a background check and some kind of behavioral analysis on a candidate (in a key role with access to sensitive data and systems), and have hired them, what next?

Continuous Monitoring and Behavioral Reassessment

This is where your HR folks earn their corn. Behavioral assessment shouldn't end with the hiring process, because stress and outside influences do not either. Continuous

monitoring and reassessment over time can help identify behavioral changes that may signal disgruntlement or stress - key risk factors for insider threats. This can be part of an insider threat program that includes:
- Ongoing assessments: Employees in sensitive roles should be periodically re-evaluated, especially after major life events (like job loss, demotion, or personal financial issues) that could trigger risky behavior.
- Monitoring behavior patterns: Behavioral analytics tools can monitor employee activity and detect potential red flags, such as increased access to sensitive systems without need or behavioral changes in system interactions.

What we've covered so far is mostly retrospective (did they do anything bad before) or 'point in time' (does their personality make us think they're OK doing bad today). What about when life happens, and people struggle to cope all of a sudden? This changes day to day, and some days can affect people more than others. We are human after all, with all our flaws, imperfections, overactive brains, personal relationships, peer pressure, social media and chemical imbalances.

Promoting Mental Health Awareness

Promoting mental health awareness in critical infrastructure entities is crucial due to the high-stress environments and the immense responsibility placed on employees. People working in sectors like energy, transportation, healthcare, schools and utilities often face intense pressure, long hours, dealing with other humans and high-stakes situations that can affect mental health and, consequently, job performance. Here are some considerations for helping these people, which (you could say callously) means reducing the risk to ourselves and our critical infrastructure operations:

(The Legal bit: Ensure that all mental health initiatives comply with legal standards - such as HIPAA or GDPR - especially concerning the privacy of employees' mental health information.)

Create a Supportive Culture.

A workplace culture that actively encourages open discussions about mental health is essential for reducing stigma. Leaders and managers should normalize conversations around mental health and well-being.
- Encourage leadership to openly talk about mental health in meetings, newsletters, and emails, showing that it's a priority at all levels of the organization.
- Run internal awareness campaigns (e.g., Mental Health Awareness Month) to educate employees about mental health issues, recognizing symptoms, and available support.
- Encourage practices like flexible working hours, time off, and workload management to help alleviate stress.
- Create anonymous channels through which employees can report stress, anxiety, or bullying in the workplace.
- Recognize that mental health is part of overall wellness, and addressing physical health, diet, exercise, and social well-being also contributes to mental resilience. Establish wellness rooms where employees can take a break to de-stress during the workday, particularly during critical moments. Offer on-site fitness programs or subsidize gym memberships to encourage physical activity, which is proven to reduce stress and improve mental health. Provide healthy food options in cafeterias and promote the benefits of balanced nutrition for mental clarity and energy. Encourage mindfulness practices, offering meditation sessions or yoga classes during or after work hours.

Monitor Stress and Burnout in High-Stress Roles.
Employees in critical infrastructure roles often face unique

stressors, including extended working hours, emergency response duties, and high levels of responsibility.
- Conduct stress and burnout assessments during performance reviews or as part of annual health check-ups.
- Where possible, implement shift rotations or offer time off to prevent burnout in employees working in high-pressure roles like cybersecurity teams, engineers, or control room operators.
- Offer specific mental health days as part of paid leave policies, allowing employees to take a break when feeling overwhelmed.

Training and Education. Empower employees and managers with knowledge about mental health so they can recognize signs of distress and know how to respond appropriately.
- Train employees to identify signs of mental health struggles in their colleagues and offer immediate support. Mental health first responders should be available in high-stress environments.
- Conduct regular mental health workshops covering topics like stress management, mindfulness, coping mechanisms, and burnout prevention.
- Create peer networks where employees can discuss challenges or stress anonymously. These can be facilitated through support groups or mentorship programs.

Employee Assistance Programs (EAP). Provide employees with easy access to mental health professionals and services when needed.
- Offer EAPs that provide confidential access to professional counseling, therapy, or psychological support for both work-related and personal issues.
- Set up a 24/7 helpline or virtual counseling services to ensure employees can reach mental health professionals outside of business hours.

- Integrate mental health apps (like Headspace or Calm) into wellness programs to help employees manage stress and anxiety through meditation and mindfulness.

Post-Incident Support. Employees involved in high-stakes incidents (e.g., dealing with security breaches, major system failures, or disaster recovery) may experience acute stress or post-traumatic stress. What if ransomware recovery was unsuccessful and a multi-$M ransom had to be paid. Or worse, the company lost millions as a result of the breach?
- After a critical incident, provide psychological debriefing sessions where employees can discuss their experiences with professional counselors.
- Monitor employees who have been involved in stressful events and offer follow-up counseling or wellness checks in the weeks following the incident.
- Implement resilience training to help employees manage stress and recover more quickly after intense work-related events.

I'll be honest, I'm a Gen-X-er so my generation was brought up to work hard and 'just get on with it'. However, then life happened to me. Due to major life incidents and stress, I have found myself spiraling into depression on more than one occasion, so I know how this feels - and it sucks. I suffer from occasional anxiety which can also be debilitating, and it comes and goes seemingly on its own schedule. On average I take about one mental health day a month. I believe the stigma is mostly gone now, but if you do find yourself in a position where you need to speak to someone, I am happy to be that someone. I am not qualified to offer professional help, but I'm a great listener. Whoever you choose, don't suffer in silence, a problem shared really is a problem halved.

Chapter 6 – Process

Probably the least sexy, least interesting chapter of the book. That's my personal opinion anyway, some weird folks live for this stuff. I've heard this called 'necessary evil' (might have even called it that myself) and other awful names. But. Having the right processes, policies and procedures (the latter two get bundled in under 'Process', let's call it 'PPP' from now on) in place can quite literally save your ass (arse if you're British). And if you're in the business of critical infrastructure, that could mean also saving the ass of many, many people. So, buckle up, grab a coffee, and let's plough through this.

Assuming you're starting from a position of zero PPP, let's talk about policy development, creation and management. And let me position this in the hierarchy of the world of PPP. I'm going to discuss the very most important, top-level PPP, I don't have the time or space to get into the minutia of PPP, plus much of that would be specific to your operating context. Have a look at the policy requirements of NIST as an example, you'll get your list.

Creating Comprehensive Critical Infrastructure Safety Policies

Effective policy development and implementation is key to ensuring that safety, security, and operational guidelines are not only set but also enforced and adapted over time to meet evolving risks and regulatory standards. When dealing with critical infrastructure, such as utilities, transportation systems, and energy grids, this process takes on even greater importance due to the potential for disruptions to public services and national security risks.

Developing a comprehensive infrastructure safety policy is the foundation of any risk management or security strategy. We covered Risk Assessment in Chapter 1. This process involves outlining clear guidelines to manage both operational and security risks and establishing protocols to ensure the safety of the workforce, infrastructure, and systems. Here are the main initial steps you'd want to consider – there are many different considerations, hence the copious use of bullets. I'm sorry, not pretty, but effective:

Identify Core Infrastructure Risks - SEE CHAPTER 1 !
- Assess physical and cybersecurity vulnerabilities.
- Include environmental hazards (natural disasters), insider threats, and potential cyber-attacks (e.g., ransomware or malware attacks on SCADA systems).

Establish Clear Objectives:
- Define the purpose of the policy, which should be to protect critical assets, ensure business continuity, and safeguard public safety.
- Align objectives with industry standards like NIST (National Institute of Standards and Technology), ISO 27001 for cybersecurity, or OSHA for workplace safety.

Role Assignment and Responsibilities:
- Clearly define the roles of policy stakeholders, such as the incident response team, cybersecurity experts, facility managers, and emergency personnel. This ensures accountability and ensures everyone understands their role in executing the policy.

Operational and Contingency Planning:
- Create business continuity plans (BCPs) that ensure operations can continue with minimal downtime even during emergencies. Note – BCP is owned by the business, Disaster Recovery (DR) is owned by the IT leadership. You'll want a DR plan too.
- Develop incident response protocols for physical intrusions, cyber breaches, or natural disasters. See section on Incident Response Plan (IRP)

Employee Training and Awareness:
- Regularly train employees on policy updates, ensuring that they are aware of their role in security and safety. This includes cybersecurity hygiene (e.g., phishing awareness) and emergency response procedures. Tabletop exercises from an Incident response perspective are particularly useful.

Next, and as you tackle the above, you'll want to think about and ensure Compliance with National and Local Regulations, because critical infrastructure entities have no choice but to comply. These regulations are designed to protect the public and ensure that vital services remain operational and secure from both physical and cyber threats.

Understanding Applicable Regulations:
- National Standards: Depending on the country, critical infrastructure is often governed by national standards. In the U.S., this includes:
    - **NERC-CIP** (North American Electric Reliability Corporation Critical Infrastructure Protection) for energy sectors.
    - **FERC** (Federal Energy Regulatory Commission) standards.
    - **HIPAA** (Health Insurance Portability and Accountability Act) for healthcare systems.
    - **GDPR** (General Data Protection Regulation) in the EU for data privacy but including EU citizens in the US.
- Local Codes and Ordinances: Beyond national regulations, local authorities may have building codes, safety standards, or data protection rules that must be adhered to.

Compliance Audits:
- Regular internal and external audits should be conducted to ensure that the policies are in line with

national and local regulations. For example, NIST recommends organizations to perform self-assessments regularly using its Cybersecurity Framework (CSF). These are useful when it comes to assessments performed by external auditors or third parties.

Collaboration with Regulatory Bodies:
- Stay in touch with relevant regulatory bodies to ensure the organization is compliant with new or updated standards. This collaboration is particularly important for sectors like energy and transportation, where government oversight is rigorous. You may well have a Chief Risk Officer or head of Compliance – this is a job for them.

Penalties and Risks of Non-Compliance:
- Failing to comply with regulations can result in financial penalties, litigation, or even operational shutdowns. Ensuring compliance helps mitigate risks associated with non-compliance, including reputation damage and legal consequences.

The dynamic nature of both physical and cyber threats means that safety policies must be regularly reviewed and updated to stay relevant. This is particularly important for critical infrastructure sectors that face rapidly evolving threats. This is what you'll want to do:

Periodic Risk Assessments:
- Conduct regular risk assessments (Chapter 1, anyone?) to identify new vulnerabilities, particularly as new technologies are implemented (e.g., IoT devices or cloud-based SCADA systems).
- Use this data to update safety policies based on real-time threat intelligence and lessons learned from incidents.

Policy Review Cycles:

- Set a defined schedule for policy reviews (e.g., annually or biannually). Review periods may also be triggered by significant events such as regulatory changes, cyber-attacks, or technological upgrades. Include cross-functional teams (IT, legal, operations, security) in these reviews to ensure that policies are comprehensive and reflect the input of all relevant stakeholders.

Incorporating Lessons Learned from Incidents:
- After any major incident, whether a cyber-attack or physical breach, conduct a post-incident analysis to evaluate how well the existing policies mitigated the threat.
- Update policies based on the findings, especially if there were gaps in response protocols or unexpected vulnerabilities in the system.

Staying Informed on Industry Standards:
- Critical infrastructure entities should keep track of emerging trends in the industry, including changes in regulatory frameworks, advances in technology, and new threat vectors.
- Regularly consult industry guidelines, such as NIST, ISO 27001, and CISA advisories, to ensure that safety policies are in alignment with the latest best practices.

Emergency Preparedness and Response

Critical infrastructure has a huge target on its back - the clue is in the title. There is no bigger statement the bad guys can make than to disrupt another nations critical infrastructure. The more lives they can make miserable, the better. And by bad guys I don't just mean antagonistic nation states or terrorist organizations – anyone with a massive grudge wants to make as big a point as possible. I've also spoken about accidents and negligence, and I haven't even mentioned natural disasters. Whatever the cause, and there are many, the effect can be catastrophic. And it always flows downhill to we, the people.

The book so far has spoken mainly about prevention – proactive technology, AI and behavioral analysis, even background checks. But given the breadth of types of doo-doo that could hit the fan, it's at this point we have to prepare for the worst, and I would argue that emergency preparedness and response policies, plans and procedures are among the most important you'll ever write, and hopefully regularly test. Because when natural disasters, cyber-attacks, or other emergencies strike, having a solid plan in place ensures the organization can minimize damage (and impact), protect personnel, and restore normal operations as quickly as possible.

Emergency Response Plan
An ERP outlines the procedures and steps that organizations should follow in the event of an emergency. For critical infrastructure, this will involve responding to cyber-attacks, natural disasters, industrial accidents, or security breaches.
- Risk Assessment: The first step in developing an ERP is conducting a thorough risk assessment. This involves identifying the most likely threats (e.g., cyber-attacks, power outages, floods, earthquakes) and understanding their potential impacts on operations. Now you would have realized why I covered this topic at the very start and repeated it a couple of times.
- Incident Command Structure (ICS): Establish a clear incident command structure, designating who is in charge during different types of emergencies and outlining the responsibilities of key personnel. The ICS should also include a clear chain of command and communication protocols.
- Resource Allocation: The ERP should detail how resources (e.g., personnel, equipment, communication tools) will be allocated and managed during an

emergency. This includes planning for backup power, spare parts, and communication tools.
- Evacuation and Shelter Plans: For physical incidents, there must be detailed evacuation routes and designated safe zones where staff and essential personnel can shelter during emergencies.
- Continuity of Operations Plan (COOP): The ERP should include a COOP to ensure that essential functions can continue during an emergency. This might involve switching to backup systems, off-site facilities, or remote work environments.

Conduct Regular Drills and Training

Emergency plans are only effective if personnel are familiar with them and capable of executing them under pressure. Regular drills and training exercises ensure that employees understand their roles and responsibilities during an emergency.
- Tabletop Exercises: These are discussion-based sessions where team members go through the steps of the emergency plan to identify gaps, improve response times, and clarify roles. Tabletop exercises simulate specific scenarios (like a cyber-attack or physical disaster) and allow team members to talk through their actions.
- Full-Scale Drills: In full-scale drills, organizations simulate real-world emergencies to test the entire emergency response plan in action. This can involve evacuations, activating backup systems, and practicing communication protocols.
- Employees from different departments (IT, security, operations) should train together to ensure seamless communication and coordination during emergencies. For instance, IT staff need to understand how their actions might affect physical security measures and vice versa.
- After each drill, conduct an AAR to evaluate performance and identify areas for improvement. This

helps refine the plan and improves response times during a real incident.

Collaboration
Working with local authorities, emergency services, and other external stakeholders is essential to ensure a coordinated response during major incidents that extend beyond the organization's internal capabilities.
- Establish MOUs with local law enforcement, fire departments, and emergency medical services to ensure that assistance can be quickly provided when needed. These agreements can also help streamline communication and resource sharing during a crisis.
- Conduct joint drills with local authorities and emergency services to practice coordinated responses to large-scale incidents. This is particularly important for incidents like natural disasters or terrorist attacks, where multiple agencies will need to work together.
- Appoint liaison officers who are responsible for communicating with external agencies during an emergency. These individuals ensure that information is shared quickly and accurately between the organization and external responders.
- Engage with the local community to ensure they are aware of the organization's emergency procedures and understand what actions they might need to take during a broader emergency (such as shelter-in-place directives or evacuation orders).

Effective communication
This is crucial during any emergency. A clear communication strategy ensures that employees, management, emergency responders, and the public are informed in a timely and accurate manner.
- Implement automated notification systems that can quickly send alerts via SMS, email, and phone to all employees, informing them of the nature of the emergency and providing instructions (e.g., evacuate, shelter in place).

- Ensure that there are reliable internal communication channels, such as radios or secure messaging apps, to coordinate between different teams during the response. Redundancy is key—ensure that backup communication systems are in place in case the primary systems fail.
- Designate a public relations officer or spokesperson to handle communication with the media and the public. Clear and accurate messaging can help mitigate panic and confusion during a crisis, while also ensuring that the organization's reputation is protected.
- Prepare pre-approved messages for different types of emergencies that can be quickly deployed in the event of a crisis. This ensures that communications are consistent, accurate, and avoid delays caused by the approval process.
- Provide clear, real-time updates to employees throughout the emergency. This includes instructions on how to respond, where to go, and when the situation has been resolved. Post-incident communication is also crucial for recovery and morale.

That's a lot. It's still not sexy, but absolutely necessary. This topic is a superpower of ours at Stealth-ISS, from writing the policies to conducting the tabletops, so without being salesy at all, if this is overwhelming and you want to advice, or just a shoulder to cry on because it's a lot, get in touch. Shoulder services are free.

PPP Best Examples

To expand on the topic a little, below are ten major 'best practice' PPP topics related to critical infrastructure you may want to investigate further. Disclaimer – without apology I took this list straight from ChatGPT so please do your own research. Most have been mentioned already, which serves to illustrate how important they are.

1. Risk Management Processes
   - Policy: Organizations should establish a formal risk management policy that defines how they will manage cybersecurity risks to systems, assets, data, and capabilities. This includes identifying, assessing, and prioritizing risks.
   - Procedures:
     - Risk Assessments: Regularly conduct risk assessments to identify vulnerabilities and potential threats to systems and data.
     - Risk Mitigation: Develop processes to mitigate identified risks, including updating security controls or implementing new safeguards.
     - Continuous Monitoring: Establish continuous monitoring mechanisms to detect emerging risks and threats.

2. Access Control Policies
   - Policy: Organizations must have strict access control policies to ensure that only authorized personnel have access to systems and data, based on their job roles and responsibilities.
   - Procedures:
     - Least Privilege Principle: Implement a least privilege policy, ensuring that users have access only to the systems and data necessary for their tasks.
     - Multi-Factor Authentication (MFA): Use MFA to strengthen user verification and protect against unauthorized access.
     - Role-Based Access Control (RBAC): Define user roles and assign access rights accordingly, ensuring that sensitive data and systems are segmented by role.

3. Incident Response Plans

- Policy: NIST emphasizes the importance of having a formal incident response policy that outlines how an organization will handle cybersecurity incidents.
- Procedures:
    - Incident Identification and Reporting: Define the process for identifying, reporting, and categorizing cybersecurity incidents.
    - Containment and Mitigation: Develop processes to contain the spread of an attack and limit the damage caused by an incident.
    - Post-Incident Review: After an incident, conduct a post-mortem analysis to assess the effectiveness of the response and update security policies accordingly.

4. Security Awareness and Training
    - Policy: NIST recommends organizations implement a security awareness policy to train employees on cybersecurity risks and best practices.
    - Procedures:
        - Training Programs: Provide regular cybersecurity awareness training to all employees, particularly focused on phishing prevention, password management, and safe browsing.
        - Testing and Simulations: Conduct regular simulations and phishing tests to ensure employees remain vigilant and can recognize threats.
        - Updates on Emerging Threats: Keep employees updated on new threats and how they can protect themselves and the organization.

5. Data Protection and Encryption Policies
    - Policy: Establish data protection policies that ensure sensitive data is encrypted both at rest and in transit.
    - Procedures:

- Encryption Standards: Use NIST-recommended encryption algorithms (such as AES-256) to secure sensitive data.
- Backup and Recovery: Implement data backup policies and ensure that backup data is encrypted and regularly tested for integrity.
- Data Classification: Classify data based on its sensitivity and apply appropriate security controls for each class.

6. Identity and Access Management (IAM)
    - Policy: Implement identity management policies to ensure that users are properly authenticated and authorized to access systems and data.
    - Procedures:
        - User Identity Verification: Define processes for verifying the identity of users before granting access to critical systems.
        - Privileged Account Management: Establish strict controls for privileged accounts, ensuring that such accounts are monitored and secured against misuse.
        - Account Deactivation: Develop procedures to promptly deactivate user accounts when employees leave the organization or change roles.

7. Supply Chain Risk Management
    - Policy: Organizations should have a supply chain risk management policy to address cybersecurity risks that originate from third-party vendors or contractors.
    - Procedures:
        - Vendor Risk Assessments: Conduct due diligence on third-party vendors, including assessments of their cybersecurity practices.

- Supply Chain Audits: Regularly audit supply chain partners to ensure they comply with the organization's cybersecurity standards.
- Contractual Security Clauses: Include cybersecurity requirements in contracts with third-party vendors and partners.

8. Continuous Monitoring and Auditing
   - Policy: Implement a continuous monitoring policy to track and respond to security events across the organization's systems.
   - Procedures:
     - Log Monitoring and Analysis: Use security information and event management (SIEM) tools to collect and analyze logs from across the network, looking for signs of suspicious activity.
     - Vulnerability Scanning: Regularly conduct vulnerability scans to identify weaknesses in systems before attackers can exploit them.
     - Penetration Testing: Periodically conduct penetration testing to simulate attacks and test the resilience of the organization's defenses.

9. Change Management
   - Policy: NIST advises organizations to have a formal change management policy that governs how system changes are requested, reviewed, approved, and implemented.
   - Procedures:
     - Change Control Board: Establish a change control board to review and approve all changes to the IT environment.
     - Documentation and Testing: Require documentation of proposed changes and test changes in a development or staging environment before deployment.

- Rollback Procedures: Ensure that rollback procedures are in place so that changes can be undone if they cause unexpected issues.

10. Business Continuity and Disaster Recovery Plans
    - Policy: Critical infrastructure organizations must have a comprehensive business continuity and disaster recovery plan (BCDR).
    - Procedures:
        - Disaster Recovery: Ensure that critical systems and data can be recovered quickly in the event of a disruption, such as a cyber-attack, hardware failure, or natural disaster.
        - Backup Testing: Regularly test backup systems to ensure data integrity and recovery time objectives (RTOs) can be met.
        - Continuity Exercises: Conduct business continuity exercises to simulate large-scale incidents and assess the organization's ability to maintain essential operations.

Chapter 7 - Designing Secure Infrastructure Facilities

So far, as promised, we've discussed the People, Process, Technology, Governance, Risk and Compliance aspects of critical infrastructure. But what if you were tasked with designing and building something from scratch?

Clearly if you've been paying any attention at all thus far, when designing secure infrastructure facilities, whether it's a data center, office building, or industrial facility, it's crucial to address both physical and cybersecurity considerations from the ground up. As part of the design as it were. I can promise you, retrofitting security is much more expensive. Here's a comprehensive approach you should take when conceptualizing and building such facilities, with focus on topics not yet discussed (all of this feeds into the concept of Layered Security Zones, which we will cover once we've discussed the basics):

Physical Security Architecture

Site Selection
The first line of defense in secure infrastructure design is choosing a location that naturally supports security:
- Geographical Risk: The facility should be located in areas with minimal exposure to natural disasters, such as floods, earthquakes, hurricanes, or wildfires. Historical data on seismic activity, weather patterns, and environmental risks should inform the decision-making process. For example, nuclear plants and data centers are often built in areas that are less prone to seismic activity to avoid operational disruptions.
- Proximity to Critical Services: The site should be relatively close to emergency services, such as law enforcement, fire departments, and hospitals. This ensures a quick response during emergencies, whether they are security incidents or accidents.

- Transport and Supply Chain Accessibility: Easy access to transportation routes (roads, airports, railways) is crucial for moving supplies, equipment, and personnel. However, the site should not be located too close to public transportation hubs, which could increase its exposure to potential threats.
- Distance from Population Centers: Critical facilities, especially nuclear power plants or large-scale industrial sites, are often located away from dense population areas. This reduces the impact in the event of a security breach, accident, or hazardous material release.
- Cyber Considerations: The availability of secure communication networks and infrastructure for cybersecurity operations must be part of the site selection process. This is important for ensuring secure connectivity for operations that depend on real-time data and digital control systems (e.g., SCADA systems).
- Location Choice: Consider the area's crime rates, environmental risks (e.g., floods, earthquakes), and accessibility. A remote location reduces risks from public exposure but may increase response times for law enforcement.
- Fencing and Barriers: Erect solid barriers, fences, or walls that restrict unauthorized access and provide a clear boundary for the facility.
- Surveillance Systems: Implement CCTV cameras, motion detectors, and thermal imaging sensors at strategic points along the perimeter. These should be integrated into the broader facility's security network and monitored 24/7.
- Access Points: Control entry points using biometric access control, smart cards, and multi-factor authentication for personnel. Vehicle barriers (e.g., bollards) should be placed at key entry points to mitigate risks from vehicular attacks.

Perimeter Security

Once the site is selected, perimeter security serves as the first line of defense against unauthorized access. OK, yes, I said people are our first line of defense, but that's in existing operations. We're talking about something net new here. Effective perimeter security requires multiple layers of protection, designed to deter, detect, and delay intruders while allowing sufficient time for a response. Key perimeter security features include:

- Fencing and Barriers: A critical first step in physical security, fences and barriers provide a visible and physical deterrent to intruders. High-security facilities often use barbed wire, electrified fences, or anti-climb walls. For nuclear sites or other sensitive areas, blast-resistant walls may be used to mitigate the effects of an external attack or explosion. Vehicle Barriers: Facilities vulnerable to vehicle-borne threats (e.g., truck bombs) often use bollards, concrete barriers, or moats around entrances to prevent unauthorized vehicles from getting too close.
- Access Control Points (Entry/Exit): Facilities must control all points of entry and exit, ensuring that only authorized personnel and vehicles can gain access. This often involves using security gates, turnstiles, and guard stations where IDs and access credentials are verified. Smart access systems, such as biometric readers or RFID cards, can further enhance security.
- Surveillance and Monitoring: CCTV cameras, thermal imaging, and drone surveillance are commonly used to monitor the perimeter in real-time. Modern systems often use AI-powered analytics to detect unusual patterns, such as loitering or unauthorized vehicles approaching the perimeter. For example, high-security data centers and government buildings frequently use motion sensors and infrared cameras to detect any unusual movements around the perimeter.
- Lighting and Landscaping: Proper lighting around the perimeter is essential for both deterring intruders and supporting surveillance systems. Motion-activated floodlights and constant illumination help reduce blind

spots. Landscaping should also be considered; clear sightlines from the facility to the perimeter are essential for spotting potential intruders, and trees or bushes that could conceal attackers should be avoided.
- Patrols and Security Personnel: Even with high-tech systems, human patrols are often necessary for robust perimeter security. Armed guards or security personnel may regularly patrol the area, especially near sensitive zones. Security personnel should be trained to respond to both physical breaches and suspicious digital activity (e.g., tampering with security systems).
- Layered Security: We'll get to this in more detail but implement multiple layers of security from the outer perimeter to inner restricted zones. This approach, often called defense in depth, includes not just fencing but also electronic surveillance, buffer zones, and physical barriers closer to critical areas. For example, nuclear facilities and government installations often include multiple fences with a buffer zone (clear zone) between them, making it difficult for intruders to approach unnoticed.

Advanced Perimeter Technologies
- Drone Detection Systems: With the rise of drones, facilities need to implement drone detection and mitigation technologies to prevent drones from breaching airspace. Some facilities use jamming devices or drone nets to neutralize unauthorized drones.
- Laser and Infrared Sensors: High-tech perimeter defense systems may include laser or infrared sensors placed along the fence line or critical points. These sensors can detect an intruder by detecting motion, heat, or body mass.
- Ground Sensors: Facilities such as nuclear plants and data centers may deploy underground pressure sensors or fiber optic cables to detect vibrations or disturbances near the perimeter, which can alert security teams to potential intrusions.

- Sonar – we covered this Chapter 2.

Physical Layer Security
This layer focuses on protecting the physical assets and people within the facility.
- Building Access Control: Use smart locks, keycards, or biometrics for door entry, and segment access based on employee roles and responsibilities.
- Hardened Structures: For critical infrastructure (e.g., data centers, control rooms), construct the facility using reinforced materials, such as concrete walls and steel doors, to withstand both physical breaches and environmental hazards.
- Internal Surveillance: Place security cameras and motion detectors inside the facility, especially near high-risk areas such as server rooms or storage areas containing sensitive equipment.

Emergency Preparedness and Redundancy
Disasters - whether natural or man-made - are inevitable. The facility should be designed to minimize downtime and continue functioning during emergencies.
- Power Redundancy: Ensure a robust power backup system is in place, such as uninterruptible power supplies (UPS) and generator systems that can provide energy during outages.
- Fire Suppression Systems: Install automatic fire suppression systems in critical areas like server rooms or electrical control centers.
- Evacuation Plans and Safe Rooms: Design the building with evacuation routes and emergency exits, as well as safe rooms where personnel can shelter during an emergency.

Layered Security Zones:

The idea here is to create multiple zones with increasing levels of security as you move closer to sensitive areas. For instance, the outer perimeter might allow public access, while interior zones require higher access privileges, with escalating levels of security.

Layered security zones are based on the idea of defense-in-depth, which means that no single point of failure should compromise the entire system. By dividing a facility into different security zones, each with increasing security measures, organizations can control and monitor access more effectively. The innermost layers contain the most sensitive assets, and access to these areas is highly restricted.

Types of Security Zones
- Outer Zone (Public Zone): The first layer includes areas that are accessible to the general public or lower-level employees. Security measures here are relatively basic, such as fences, gates, security cameras, and patrols. This zone could include visitor areas, parking lots, or lobbies.
- Controlled Zone: This zone requires higher access control mechanisms such as badge systems, turnstiles, or visitor sign-ins. It may also involve human guards checking credentials. Only authorized personnel can enter these areas. This is common for administrative offices or less critical workspaces.
- Restricted Zone: Only vetted employees with specific roles are allowed into this area, which houses important but non-critical assets. Additional measures may include biometric access controls (e.g., fingerprint or facial recognition) and constant surveillance.
- Sensitive Zone: This area contains critical systems or confidential information, such as servers, control rooms, or areas where radioactive materials are handled in nuclear plants. Access is severely limited to only high-clearance personnel, and multiple layers of identification (e.g., MFA, biometric scans, and security clearance checks) are required.
- Core or Critical Zone: The innermost zone is the most secure, containing the highest-value assets, such as

nuclear reactor controls, critical systems, or sensitive data repositories. Access to this zone is extremely restricted, and it may include armed guards, motion detectors, pressure sensors, and 24/7 monitoring. Any attempt to breach this zone usually triggers immediate alarms and a rapid security response.

Security Measures by Zone
- Surveillance: The outer zones might use standard CCTV cameras, while inner zones use high-definition, thermal, or AI-enhanced surveillance systems that can detect abnormal behavior or unauthorized access.
- Access Controls: Each zone will have increasingly sophisticated access control mechanisms. For example, the public zones may only have ID badges, while the most restricted zones require multi-factor authentication (MFA) using biometrics and smart cards.
- Guards and Patrols: The outer zones may have periodic patrols or unarmed guards, while the innermost zones often feature armed security personnel trained to respond to any potential breaches.
- Physical Barriers: Barriers like fences, bollards, reinforced doors, and blast walls become more prominent as you move from the outer to the inner zones. Each barrier is designed to delay intruders and provide time for the response teams to take action.

Benefits of Layered Security Zones

For me the primary benefit is Risk Mitigation: If one layer is breached, the intruder is delayed by the next, providing time for security teams to intervene. This minimizes the risk of a full-scale compromise of sensitive areas.

Then, Early Detection: Each layer provides opportunities to detect intrusions. Alarms, motion sensors, and surveillance in outer zones can trigger early warnings before intruders reach sensitive areas.

These are supported by the fact that Role-Based Access Control (RBAC) is 'easy' with layered zones, and organizations can assign access rights based on job roles. For example, administrative staff might only have access to controlled zones, while engineers may access the restricted zone. Each zone's security can also be tailored to its risk level. Lower-risk zones might only require basic security measures, while high-risk zones need a combination of physical, electronic, and human-based controls.

Convergence and Layers (Integration of Cyber and Physical Security)

This was covered in more detail in Chapter 4 but is repeated here for completeness of this chapter. As critical infrastructure increasingly integrates cybersecurity measures with physical security, a reminder that layered security zones must account for both:

- Network Segmentation: Similar to physical zones, network segmentation divides systems into zones with strict access controls. The most critical systems (e.g., ICS, SCADA systems) should reside in highly restricted zones isolated from public or lower-security networks.
- Converged Security Operations Centers (SOC): Combining physical and cyber threat monitoring, SOCs ensure that physical security incidents (such as an intruder entering the restricted zone) and cyber incidents (such as attempts to hack into the control systems) are addressed together.

Other

Topics covered already by listed here for completeness of this chapter:

- XDR

- Monitoring and Incident Response
- AI and ML
- Compliance and Legal Considerations
- Industry Standards
- Data Privacy Laws
- Regular Security Audits

Site selection and perimeter security are integral to the overall defense strategy of critical infrastructure facilities. Choosing a secure location that minimizes exposure to risks, combined with a multi-layered perimeter defense, ensures that both physical and cyber threats are deterred and neutralized before reaching the most critical assets. By leveraging modern surveillance technologies, access control mechanisms, and real-time monitoring, organizations can protect their infrastructure from a wide range of threats, including natural disasters, cyber-attacks, and physical intrusions. Safe to say, the more you invest in the analysis, the better your choice (assuming you act on the results) and the lower your risk.

Chapter 8 –Safety Considerations Today

Let's take this opportunity to discuss the current state of play (2024), to try to show how everything discussed so far is completely relevant, with a view to thinking forwards. (The Future will be the next chapter.) As mentioned in the introduction, CISA lists 16 critical infrastructure sectors. I would argue, and I'm happy to have a discussion about it, that the generation of electricity is the component that impacts them all. (Communication/Internet comes a close second, but that needs electricity to operate, right?). If a bad actor wanted to cause maximum damage, it stands to reason they would try to impact power generation and distribution (the grid). Cast your mind back to 2015/6 – hackers twice caused power outages in Ukraine.

We've covered two of the threat vectors in some detail in this book – physical attacks and cybersecurity attacks. When it comes to anything electrical, there is a third, almost existential threat – Electronic Magnetic Pulses (EMPs). These can be and are generated from geomagnetic flares, or worse, from a terrorist missile exploded in the atmosphere. I say worse because flares are 'natural', missiles are intentional, and the world probably has bigger problems to deal with at that point in time. Assuming our governments are doing their best to protect us from EMPs, much as the suggestions in this book can't do much more than that, we can't ignore the need for policies, procedures, training, emergency and contingency planning, can we?

Nuclear

The subset of power generation that gets people most excited is nuclear. High-value target, that's for sure. So, let's focus on that. Taking a coal fired power station offline is one thing, messing with a nuclear power plant could lead to a whole extra world of hurt. Look at the impact of the Fukushima, Japan, disaster in 2011. And that was 'natural causes'. There are many well-known examples of nuclear disasters. Whatever the cause, the impact can be horrific.

The world of nuclear power generation is advancing quite significantly. Consider the major datacenter or 'cloud' companies and their never-ending thirst for power. Consider the need for localized power as the population expands, and as we decommission those fossil fuel plants, or they become obsolete. Don't forget governments keen on getting to 'Net Zero' (not covering that here, whole different topic) by switching off fossil-fueled facilities. Nuclear answers these questions. There's a huge market for developing the concept of Small Modular Reactors (SMRs). Also, further down the pipeline are Advanced Modular Reactors (AMRs). SMRs are interesting because they are designed such that they can be fabricated in a factory environment and transported to site. Great from a cost, time and flexibility perspective, but how are these to be secured?

The point is, expect to see a proliferation and increased reliance on nuclear power. Add the current situation – legacy and ageing nuclear infrastructure. Now think about the potential downside of compromise, or accident, or act of God (many Gods are available). So, from the perspective of safety and security, aren't we just increasing the size of the attack surface? Yes, it seems we are, thanks for asking. Here's a sample of how the powers-that-be are figuring this out:

Security and Safeguards in SMRs

- "Nuclear Security and Safeguards for Small Modular Reactors" by the World Nuclear Association - Discusses the unique security and safeguards

challenges SMRs pose, particularly in terms of proliferation resistance.
- "Security of Nuclear Facilities: The Role of Small Modular Reactors" by Nuclear Threat Initiative (NTI) - Focuses on the security demands and the international framework for securing SMRs.

Regulatory and Policy Aspects

- "Regulatory Perspectives on SMRs" by the Canadian Nuclear Safety Commission (CNSC) - A look at how Canada is regulating the safety and security of SMRs.
- "Small Modular Reactors: Licensing and Regulatory Issues" by the U.S. Nuclear Regulatory Commission (NRC) - Outlines the specific licensing and security considerations for SMR deployment in the U.S.

SMRs and Non-Proliferation

- "Non-Proliferation and Small Modular Reactors: Ensuring a Secure Energy Future" by the Carnegie Endowment for International Peace - Examines how SMRs can be made proliferation-resistant.

Fascinating reading. Side note from our nuclear safety advisor – Paddy Parvin: "If someone fiddles with it (SMR), the risk of an explosion is extraordinarily low if not impossible. However, there is scope for it to be overworked, leading to power and hence core thermal criteria limits to be breached. This would lead to partial or even total core melt, that would render the unit inoperable. That doesn't mean that radiation won't be released, you just need to have pressure surge contingency – embedded in the design is the requirement under law for a containment building. Pressure surges could be delivered by dissociation of water and hydrogen burn, but a true nuclear weapon yield cannot happen owing to the low levels of Uranium enrichment deployed. It's how they're designed. But they can make people sick or worse long-term if tampered with – this circles back to robust regulation and robust security."

Can we agree that everything discussed in this book so far is still relevant when it comes to protecting nuclear power generation facilities? Layered/zoned defenses, XDR, all of that? Here are some emerging considerations, specific to SMRs, that have relevance to wider areas of critical infrastructure in the future – see if you can spot the theme:

Enhanced Physical Security by Design
As Paddy noted above, SMRs are designed with inherent safety features that can also contribute to physical security. Many SMR designs are smaller, potentially allowing for underground placement or more secure, compact configurations. This can reduce the risk of external attacks or sabotage by making key components less accessible. For example, some SMR designs have reduced external cooling requirements, decreasing the number of vulnerable external systems that could be targeted in an attack. The point here is, we should be considering the wider design of entire systems, not just specific components. I've said it before, we are all as strong as our weakest link. As a specialist security company, we always recommend our clients design in security at the outset of all their projects. From experience I can assure you that the cost of preventative cybersecurity is about 1/20 the cost of breach. As my mum used to say, a penny of prevention is worth a pound of cure.

Distributed Deployment
SMRs are intended to be deployed in multiple, smaller sites rather than centralized at a single massive plant. While this reduces the risk of a catastrophic event at a single location, it creates a more distributed network of facilities to protect (larger attack surface), potentially increasing the overall physical and cybersecurity burden. The challenge is that more sites mean more locations to

secure from both physical and cyber threats, and smaller plants might not always have the same robust on-site security as larger facilities. Over the years I've seen organizations move from centralized operations to decentralized and back again. I guess it's a function of external market forces and (more cynically) new leadership over time needing to be seen to be doing something different, which turns into industry trends. Both 'destinations' have their pros and cons. My point is both 'destinations' need a strong physical and cybersecurity strategy and design (see first point) when it comes to security.

Cybersecurity Challenges
Like all modern critical infrastructure, SMRs are vulnerable to cyberattacks. The digital systems used to control these reactors, such as SCADA (Supervisory Control and Data Acquisition) systems, could be targeted by cyber adversaries. The smaller footprint of SMRs means their cyber defenses must be as robust as those of larger facilities, even though their digital architecture may differ. Which brings us back to security by design – we must ensure the control systems of SMRs are isolated from non-critical networks and constantly monitored for anomalies to prevent hacking or manipulation.

Opportunities for New Security Technologies
SMRs present an opportunity to integrate modern security technologies such as AI-powered surveillance systems, automated drones for perimeter monitoring, and advanced sensor systems for early detection of threats. These technologies can be woven into the modular design of SMRs to create a more secure operational environment.

Opportunities to Reduce National Security Risk
America's aging grid threatens national security. The United States' power grid is often referred to as the "largest machine" in the country, but it is also aging and increasingly vulnerable. Originally designed decades ago,

much of the grid's infrastructure is outdated, under-maintained, and was never meant to handle the demands of modern energy consumption or threats posed by climate change and cybersecurity risks. Electric vehicle mandates anyone? Upgrading could not only reduce risk but also cost - the cost of maintaining the outdated infrastructure is high, and frequent outages harm the economy. The new infrastructure including SMRs would arguably be better protected against physical and cyberattack than the legacy infrastructure. Assuming the design is right.

For completeness here are some considerations specific to the nuclear industry, that are interesting and may help put your mind at rest a little and give more examples as to why they are a good idea – there may even be lessons for the future:

Reduced Radioactive Material Handling
Specific to the topic of nuclear but traditional reactors require regular refueling and handling of large amounts of radioactive material, increasing the risk of theft or diversion. SMRs, however, often operate for much longer without refueling (sometimes 10-15 years), limiting opportunities for adversaries to access fissile material.

Regulatory Adaptation
SMRs require new security regulations to account for their unique characteristics. I noted a few of these in the section above. Traditional nuclear facilities are governed by strict security frameworks that may not always align with the size and distributed nature of SMRs. Governments and international bodies like the IAEA (International Atomic Energy Agency) and NTI have been working on updating these frameworks to include SMRs. All intended change in the world of critical infrastructure needs new regulation.

Resilience Against Natural and Human-Induced Disasters

The smaller, more contained nature of SMRs can make them more resilient to both natural disasters (such as earthquakes and floods) and human-induced disasters (such as terrorist attacks or acts of war). Their often-underground placement can make them harder to target, and the modular design could allow for quicker replacement or repair in the event of damage.

Economic and Logistical Considerations
SMRs have a smaller physical footprint and lower upfront capital costs compared to large nuclear plants, which can make them more attractive to smaller energy providers. Additionally, SMRs can be modular, so companies build what they need now, and add as demand dictates. However, the trade-off may be that smaller operators might not have the same resources for comprehensive physical and cyber security measures. As a result, security requirements must be balanced with economic feasibility.

Military Bases – Smart Bases

It's national security, stupid! (Plagiarized and adapted from Jim Carville, 1992.) But given that the warrior of the future (current?) is a 17-year-old living in their regime's basement with a keyboard for a weapon, how are the military machine and national security departments evolving to counter this threat?

Military bases are having to evolve rapidly to address modern threats like the new techno-warrior, but also technological advancements, convergence, and the complexities of global defense operations. This transformation encompasses both physical infrastructure and cybersecurity measures, driven by the increasing reliance on digital systems and the evolving nature of warfare and associated sensitive data. The integration of advanced technologies like artificial intelligence (AI), Internet of Things (IoT), drones, and enhanced communication systems is reshaping how military bases operate and protect themselves from both physical and cyber threats.

Military bases today are no longer just glorified storage depots housing troops, vehicles, and equipment. They are having to become digital fortresses that integrate real-time intelligence, advanced automation, and networked capabilities. Command and control systems are the heart of military operations, allowing leaders to communicate with troops, deploy resources, and coordinate actions. The increasing reliance on networked systems means these systems must be protected from cyberattacks that could disrupt communication, disable defenses, or manipulate military actions. A cyberattack on a base's command system could prevent troops from receiving orders, disrupt logistics, or even alter intelligence to mislead decision-makers. Already in place are safeguards like restricted access, secure document handling, secure communications, behavioral monitoring and analysis and supply chain security. But some key evolutions include:

Smart Bases
Military bases are adopting smart technologies, similar to smart cities, where sensors, IoT devices, and AI are being used to monitor and control everything from energy consumption to logistics and security systems. These smart bases allow for better operational efficiency, but they also create new attack surfaces for cyber threats. For example, smart energy grids on bases optimize power usage and ensure backup power during outages, but their reliance on IoT devices makes them vulnerable to cyberattacks.

Autonomous Systems and Robotics
The deployment of autonomous systems like drones, ground robots, and unmanned vehicles has significantly enhanced the security and operational capabilities of bases. These systems can patrol perimeters, monitor for physical threats, and even engage targets if necessary.

However, they also introduce complex challenges in ensuring secure communication and preventing hacking or takeover by adversaries.

Virtual Operations Centers
The increased reliance on virtual operations centers (sometimes known as digital twin bases, which we covered earlier) is an emerging trend. These centers allow remote management of base operations, enabling leaders to monitor and control physical and digital aspects of the base from afar. This reduces the number of personnel required on-site but increases the need for secure, resilient communications networks.

The physical security of military bases remains critical, even as digital threats increase. Evolving physical security measures must now integrate both traditional security tactics and emerging technologies:

Perimeter Security
Physical perimeter defenses are being enhanced with automated monitoring through sensors, cameras, radar, LiDAR, and AI-driven analytics. Bases can detect intrusions or threats in real-time, often before they cross the perimeter. A base equipped with AI-driven facial and license plate recognition can monitor incoming personnel or vehicles for potential threats, identifying unauthorized access attempts more quickly and efficiently than traditional human checkpoints.

Hardened Infrastructure
As bases become more digital, their physical infrastructure needs to be hardened to withstand both traditional and cyber-physical attacks. This includes reinforcing physical structures, securing critical infrastructure like energy systems, and ensuring redundancy in communications and power. For example, bases are hardening their power grids to protect against both EMP (electromagnetic pulse)

attacks and cyberattacks, ensuring that critical systems remain operational during an attack.

Defending Against Drones

The proliferation of drones, especially as a potential threat from adversaries, means that bases are now deploying anti-drone technologies such as jamming systems, pilot identification and location, laser weapons, drone capture and kinetic interception. I'd love to write a book on this topic alone, and tell some stories about what we are doing with various government agencies and even major casino resorts to combat this growing nuisance/threat. Homemade 'nonstandard' ghost drones are a thing, look it up.

As military bases modernize, cybersecurity becomes increasingly crucial. The shift towards more connected and digitalized operations has created vulnerabilities that could be exploited by nation-states, terrorist groups, or other malicious actors. Here's what's happening in the context of military bases, which reinforces much of what we have discussed already:

Defending Against Cyber-Physical Attacks

We agree military bases like all critical infrastructure are vulnerable to cyber-physical attacks. The good news is that, assuming government agencies all on the same side and are willing, the sheer volume of threat intel available is off the charts. Add in private sector intel and it's truly staggering. That causes its own problems though – how do you sort through that amount of data, and how do you determine which threats are credible? Well, AI and ML - below. Layer this in with continuous monitoring and a zoned/layered architecture and some network segmentation and you probably have enough to thwart any determined attacker.

AI and Machine Learning Defenses

These are being integrated into military cybersecurity systems to detect and respond to threats faster than human operators can. These systems can analyze vast amounts of data, detect anomalies, and respond to attacks in real-time. Covered earlier if you want more detail.

Insider Threats - The growing complexity of digital operations means that insider threats - either intentional or accidental - pose significant risks. Personnel with access to key systems could intentionally compromise security or be manipulated into revealing sensitive information through social engineering or phishing attacks. Those personnel may even have their fingers on the triggers of something destructive. Like an armed drone somewhere in the world. Food for thought for sure. Check out the chapter on 'People', there are many suggestions there as to how to lower this particular risk.

Training and Simulations
Military bases are also increasingly conducting cyber wargames and simulations to prepare for potential cyberattacks. These exercises help personnel respond more effectively and quickly during an actual cyber incident, reducing downtime and mitigating damage.

From the above you can see it's crucial that military bases adopt a holistic, defense-in-depth design and strategy that integrates both cyber and physical security measures to safeguard operations in this increasingly complex environment. Guessing you knew that's where I was going here.

Schools

Schools today face a broad array of both current and emerging risks, spanning across physical security, cybersecurity, environmental and mental health concerns. These risks are evolving rapidly due to societal changes, technological advancements, and shifts in the global threat landscape. Putting things like vandalism, bullying and tornadoes to one side, in the book I'd like to focus on just two real and present dangers to schools right now, because this is a book about security: shooters, and ransomware.

Shooters

The threat of school shootings has become one of the most significant and tragic risks facing educational institutions, particularly in the United States. Columbine High School Massacre – 13 dead. Virginia tech – 32 dead, 17 wounded. Sandy Hook – 26 dead. Marjory Stoneman – 17 dead. Robb Elementary School 2022 – 21 dead. I won't go into the split between children and adults, but in the 2021-2022 school year a total of 327 shooting incidents occurred, resulting in 81 deaths and 269 injuries. Whether you believe this to be a gun control issue or a mental health issue, it's a sickening number of dead schoolchildren and educators. Every. Single. Year.

The increasing frequency of these events, combined with their devastating impact on communities, has forced schools, policymakers, law enforcement, and security experts to continually evolve their preparedness and response strategies. There would appear to be numerous motivations for committing these heinous acts, from bullying, desire for revenge and need for notoriety, through to mental health issues and access to firearms. Solutions to those are way beyond the remit of this book. However, there are some common behaviors that could be analyzed to try to get ahead of a shooting:

- Leakage: This refers to the shooter revealing their intentions or making threats in the days or weeks prior to the attack. They might do this verbally or through social media posts.

- Obsession with Violence: Many shooters show an interest in past mass shootings, violence, or weapons. They may express admiration for other shooters or consume violent content online.
- Changes in Behavior: Some shooters experience noticeable changes in behavior, such as withdrawing from friends and family, engaging in self-harm, or showing a decline in academic performance.

I'm not advocating some kind of blanket Orwellian population surveillance end case, far from it, but for the sake of our schoolchildren I am advocating the use of technology to assist those humans and communities closest to these potential perpetrators in unearthing whether these people are a threat to others, and indeed themselves.

The physical school environment brings a world of different challenges. Schools are designed to be open and welcoming environments, which can make securing them difficult. They have multiple entry points, large student populations, and frequent visitors, making it hard to control access. Many schools have open campuses with unrestricted access during certain hours. This can allow shooters to enter without raising suspicion, particularly if they are familiar with the school's layout.

What's Being Done?

How are schools evolving their security measures? We've mentioned the use of technology – digital twins and AI, CCTV, LiDAR, facial recognition, detection technologies. The problem is this technology can be expensive and not all schools can afford it, or choose to prioritize it over educational needs. Back to a penny of prevention being worth a pound of cure I suppose. That's great until your school is targeted by a shooter. That's a conversation for a different book. Anyway, here some great examples of (mostly non-technology) preventative activities that have been deployed recently (some in response to shooter incidents, others being proactive):

- **Marjory Stoneman Douglas High School** in Florida, the site of a tragic school shooting in 2018, implemented single-point entry systems, which require visitors to pass through a single, monitored access point with ID checks and security personnel. This reduces the likelihood of an outsider gaining easy access to the campus.
- Schools in **Texas** have installed gunshot detection systems, which can instantly notify law enforcement when a firearm is discharged, helping to accelerate response times and minimize casualties.
- The **Clark County School District** in Nevada, which includes Las Vegas, has a robust SRO (School Resource Officer) program where officers patrol school grounds daily, foster relationships with students, and respond rapidly to any security threats.
- **Sandy Hook Elementary School** in Newtown, Connecticut, worked closely with law enforcement after the tragic 2012 shooting to design better response protocols. Today, the school conducts regular joint exercises with law enforcement to improve coordination.
- **Los Angeles Unified School District (LAUSD)**, one of the largest in the U.S., has adopted quarterly active shooter drills in which both students and staff participate. These drills simulate real-life scenarios and help identify gaps in the school's response plan.
- The **Pasadena Independent School District** in Texas has introduced drones as part of their tactical response plan. These drones can enter school buildings and provide live footage to law enforcement during an active shooter incident, allowing for quicker, safer responses.
- **Ohio schools** have widely implemented ALICE (Alert, Lockdown, Inform, Counter, Evacuate) training, ensuring that staff and students alike are equipped with

multiple options during an active shooter scenario, giving them more tools to improve survival chances.
- After the shooting at **Parkland's Marjory Stoneman Douglas High School**, Florida passed the "Marjory Stoneman Douglas High School Public Safety Act", which mandated the creation of behavioral threat assessment teams in every school district to address potential threats through early intervention.
- In **New York City Public Schools**, mental health services have been expanded to ensure that each student has access to social workers, school psychologists, and trained counselors who can intervene when a student is at risk of harming themselves or others.
- The Safe2Tell program in **Colorado** allows students to anonymously report potential school threats via phone or app. This program has been instrumental in preventing numerous potential attacks by enabling students to voice concerns discreetly.
- In 2021, **Chicago Public Schools** received significant funding through the Department of Justice's School Violence Prevention Program (SVPP) to improve security camera systems, hire more security personnel, and enhance access control in school buildings.

Don't get me wrong, all schools are different, and none are completely passive when it comes to protecting our kids. There are now active shooter drills, armed security and much improved access and visitor management protocols. But from experience having conduced school security assessments personally, point solutions are great but 'joined up' thinking is required. It does need a multi-layered approach, and that is particularly difficult in vast, open plan campuses when the supply of funding is limited.

I'll make one last point before I move on to cybersecurity and ransomware. We as a company have worked with smart cities (all international) and their constituent components (schools and other elements of critical infrastructure) for many years. You could call the smart cities we've worked with 'benevolent dictatorships', and by that, I mean centralized decision making, control and financing. Very easy to make progress. Working in the 'West', especially in the US is totally different – decentralized everything (too many cooks) means it's difficult to make progress on anything while those 'in charge' all want their agendas to be included.

However, and this is just my observation, one thing that is common between 'east' and 'west' is the amount of collaboration with key stakeholders – us, the citizens. It seems the powers that be feel entitled to make decisions on behalf of all the citizens for their supposed greater good. And that's fine in many cases. Until it's not. That said, when it comes to our children in schools, I believe there are key groups of people that do not have equal billing. And they are the Parent Teacher Associations, the Churches, even the parents and students themselves. In the context of smart cities, schools are mini community centers, and all members of that community should have a say in the prioritization of the protection of the children. It's not all about exam pass rates, I'll leave that there.

Ransomware

Why are schools targeted by hackers? Ignoring the already rising trend pre-Covid, the COVID-19 pandemic led to a significant shift in how schools operated, with widespread adoption of remote learning tools. This transition to digital platforms made schools even more vulnerable to ransomware attacks, and by 2020, there was an explosion in the number of incidents. Remote learning created new vulnerabilities in school networks, and attackers exploited these weaknesses. Cybersecurity firms reported a 388% increase in attacks on the education sector in the second half of 2020 compared to the first half. Here's why schools are an easy target (hackers love easy targets):

- Limited Cybersecurity Resources. Many schools, especially K-12 institutions, operate on tight budgets and often do not have the resources to implement advanced cybersecurity defenses. This makes them vulnerable to ransomware attacks because their systems may not be as well protected as those in other sectors, such as finance or healthcare.
- Legacy Systems. Further to the point above, many schools rely on outdated or legacy systems that are easier to breach.
- High Value of Data, Data Exfiltration and Public Exposure. Schools store a wealth of sensitive data, including personal information about students, staff, and parents (e.g., names, addresses, Social Security numbers, and health records). Cybercriminals know that schools may be willing to pay ransoms to prevent this data from being leaked or sold on the dark web.
- Critical Disruption Potential. Ransomware can shut down school operations entirely by disabling access to critical administrative functions, online learning platforms, and communication systems. This causes significant disruption, especially in a post-pandemic world where remote learning is common. As a result, schools may feel pressured to pay the ransom quickly to restore operations. Ransom demands have also increased significantly. In the past, schools might have faced ransom demands in the tens of thousands of dollars. However, by 2021-2023, these demands had escalated to hundreds of thousands or even millions. Given the pressure to restore operations quickly, some schools feel compelled to pay, especially if they lack comprehensive backups.
- Lack of Backups and Incident Response Plans. Some schools lack robust data backup systems or do not have effective incident response plans in place. Without reliable backups, it becomes difficult to recover encrypted data, forcing schools into a difficult position where paying the ransom may seem like the only viable option.

- Lack of Awareness and Training. Both faculty and students may lack sufficient cybersecurity training, making them more vulnerable to phishing emails and other attack vectors. Superintendents and district boards may need to be better educated on the problem, and potential solutions.

Ransomware attacks on schools have become more sophisticated. Attackers now employ advanced tactics such as double extortion, where not only is the school's data encrypted, but the attackers also threaten to release sensitive data if the ransom isn't paid. This trend has been particularly prominent since 2020. Attackers increasingly use Ransomware-as-a-Service (RaaS), where they sell or rent out ransomware kits to other criminals. This has lowered the barrier to entry for launching ransomware attacks, leading to more frequent and less predictable incidents.

What's Being Done?

There has been focus on the weaknesses above as evidenced in the examples below. My only comment at this point is that funding in many cases seemed to be made available AFTER the breach:

- The **Baltimore County Public Schools** district, after suffering a ransomware attack in 2020, implemented a robust backup system. The district is now able to restore data quickly if ransomware strikes again.
- The **Clark County School District** in Nevada, after its 2020 attack, invested heavily in intrusion detection and threat monitoring tools that monitor network traffic for abnormal behavior, allowing them to detect and neutralize threats early.
- **Los Angeles Unified School District (LAUSD)**, one of the largest in the country, now conducts regular phishing simulations and has built comprehensive

training modules on how to avoid common cyber threats. This effort comes after the district faced an attempted ransomware attack.
- **Des Moines Public Schools**, after facing a ransomware incident in 2023, implemented a detailed incident response plan, which includes a step-by-step guide for isolating affected systems, communicating with law enforcement, and recovering from an attack using backup data.

In other news, the US federal government has increased funding for cybersecurity initiatives aimed at schools. Through the American Rescue Plan, millions of dollars have been allocated to help schools improve their digital defenses and recover from cyber incidents. Also, the K-12 Cybersecurity Act of 2021 requires the Department of Homeland Security to study the cyber risks facing K-12 schools and provide recommendations for enhancing their cybersecurity posture. Many school districts are now applying for federal grants through programs like the E-Rate program, which provides funding for broadband and cybersecurity improvements, especially in underserved areas.

The U.S. government, through CISA, provides detailed ransomware prevention guidelines specifically for K-12 schools. CISA offers tools like malware scanners and threat intelligence services, which help schools identify and remediate vulnerabilities before they are exploited. After the attack on Fairfield-Suisun Unified School District in California, the district collaborated with CISA and implemented recommended best practices, including a security audit, network segmentation, and endpoint monitoring.

Some schools are partnering with cybersecurity firms (just like Stealth-ISS – other firms are available) to manage and monitor their systems 24/7. Miami-Dade County Public Schools has partnered with a cybersecurity firm to deploy artificial intelligence-driven monitoring tools that track and alert IT teams of unusual network activity, helping to quickly neutralize any threat.

Some schools are investing in advanced cybersecurity training for their IT departments. This equips IT staff with the skills to manage complex threats and handle sophisticated cyberattacks. New York City Public Schools initiated advanced cybersecurity certification programs for IT personnel, helping them understand how to defend the network against the latest ransomware variants and other malware.

Finally, some schools are turning to cybersecurity insurance to mitigate the financial impact of ransomware attacks. While this doesn't prevent attacks, it provides a financial safety net for recovering costs associated with data recovery, system restoration, and ransom payments. The cost of the tarnished reputation is not covered. Texas public schools, particularly in smaller districts, have started taking out cybersecurity insurance policies that provide coverage in case of ransomware attacks, helping them recover more quickly without depleting educational resources.

Ransomware attacks on schools are likely to continue rising unless significant investments are made in cybersecurity infrastructure, training, and preventive measures. Without sounding like a broken record, schools must adopt a layered, proactive approach, including regular backups, network segmentation, and a comprehensive incident response plan, to better defend against these attacks. I'm not saying it's necessary to adopt all of the countermeasures. What I am saying is that doing nothing is no longer an option. Especially as the proliferation of hacker gangs increases, and the next one doesn't care that you paid a ransom last week, they want their money for the new hack this week.

At this point I was going to cover sporting events, commercial properties and even transportation. But for the sake of your time and mine, I think you get the point. If it's critical, we need to pay attention. List of key learnings and lessons in the concusion.

Chapter 9 – The Future

The future of physical and cybersecurity for critical infrastructure will evolve significantly across the multiple dimensions I brought up at the start: people, process, technology, and governance, risk, and compliance (GRC). As emerging threats grow more sophisticated and interconnected, organizations managing critical infrastructure - such as power grids, water supplies, bases, transportation, and healthcare systems - must adopt a holistic, multi-dimensional approach to stay resilient. Here's what the future likely holds for each of these dimensions:

People

The role of human resources in physical security will remain central, but with technological integration becoming more advanced, the human factor will shift toward more strategic roles.

- Training and Response Teams. The future will see more personnel trained in integrated cyber-physical security, with the rise of blended security forces who can handle both cyber incidents and physical breaches. These teams will require knowledge of security technology, such as drone detection, CCTV analytics, and AI-enhanced monitoring systems.
- Security Personnel and Robotics. In many critical infrastructure sectors, robotic patrols and automated systems will complement human guards. Robots equipped with cameras, sensors, and even AI algorithms will patrol facilities, report intrusions, and even respond to threats autonomously. This will reduce the need for personnel in highly dangerous areas while ensuring continuous monitoring.

- Collaboration and Insider Threat Detection. Recognizing that insiders (employees, contractors, etc.) can be a source of significant physical risk, more advanced background checks, biometric access, and behavioral monitoring will be used to detect potential insider threats. Tools to monitor employee behavior and access patterns (e.g., abnormal physical access to critical areas) will be increasingly deployed.

The human element remains one of the most important and vulnerable aspects of securing critical infrastructure from a cybersecurity perspective. The workforce will need to evolve in response to more advanced threats and the increasing reliance on technology – maybe train those displaced by AI? Just a thought:

- Training and Awareness. The workforce of the future will require continuous training in cybersecurity best practices, particularly as phishing and social engineering attacks remain a primary attack vector. Employees, from IT specialists to operational staff, must be aware of the threats they face.
- Cybersecurity Talent Shortage. As critical infrastructure increasingly relies on complex technologies, the demand for skilled cybersecurity professionals will grow. Finding and retaining this talent will be a significant challenge. The development of more specialized training programs and cybersecurity-focused education will be necessary.
- Collaborative Culture. Bridging the gap between IT and operational technology (OT) teams will be essential. Traditionally, OT teams managing physical systems and IT teams managing digital systems have operated in silos, but the integration of these two will become increasingly critical to counter cyber-physical threats. Add in physical security systems and you have real convergence.
- AI and Automation in Security. With the growing use of AI, automation will take on repetitive cybersecurity

tasks (e.g., monitoring, detection, response). This will shift the workforce focus on strategic decision-making, incident response, and system oversight rather than routine activities.

Process

The processes governing physical security will focus on greater automation and integration with cybersecurity protocols to ensure that vulnerabilities in one area do not expose the other.

- Automated Access Control and Surveillance. Processes around entry and exit points will become fully automated, with biometric access control (fingerprints, facial recognition, iris scans) linked to digital credentials. Surveillance will shift to a process-driven model, where AI-driven analytics continuously monitor real-time video feeds for anomalies (unauthorized access, suspicious behavior) and trigger immediate alerts.
- Response Processes. In the future, response procedures will become more streamlined and AI-augmented. When an intrusion is detected, incident response protocols will be automatically triggered - locking down specific areas, alerting law enforcement, and isolating critical systems to prevent sabotage. This will reduce response times and limit human error.
- Integration of Physical and Cybersecurity Protocols. Physical security processes will increasingly need to account for cyber-physical attacks, where cyber intrusions can enable physical breaches (or vice versa). For example, an attack on access control systems via malware could disable security cameras or unlock gates. Processes will involve the continuous testing of both cyber and physical safeguards through penetration testing and red-teaming.

As cyber and physical threats become more complex, robust processes must be established to ensure resilience and swift response to incidents. Key areas of focus will include:

- Incident Response Plans. The development of more sophisticated and integrated incident response plans that address both physical and cybersecurity incidents will be crucial. For instance, a ransomware attack targeting an energy grid might have physical safety implications, necessitating a unified response.
- Zero Trust Architecture. (Many people think this is a technology, but to my mind it's actually a strategy formed by a set of different connection policies, that's why it's here.) Many organizations are adopting a Zero Trust security model, where trust is never assumed, and all access must be continually verified. This process will become more common in critical infrastructure to prevent unauthorized access to both physical systems (e.g., access controls) and cyber systems.
- Supply Chain Risk Management. With critical infrastructure relying on vast and complex supply chains, there will be an increased focus on ensuring that third-party vendors and suppliers adhere to strict cybersecurity protocols. Processes for vetting, monitoring, and responding to supply chain breaches will be key.
- Integration of OT and IT Security. The convergence of IT and OT will require the creation of new security processes that account for the specific needs of both. This involves securing industrial control systems (ICS) and SCADA (Supervisory Control and Data Acquisition) systems, which were traditionally separated from IT systems.

Technology

The technology for physical security will dramatically evolve, leveraging advances in artificial intelligence (AI), Internet of Things (IoT), and drones to enhance detection, prevention, and response to physical threats.

- Smart Surveillance. Surveillance systems will become more intelligent, using AI-powered facial recognition and behavioral analysis to detect threats in real time. Cameras will no longer just record; they will interpret movements and trigger responses to suspicious activities, making security monitoring more proactive than reactive.
- Drones and Robotics. Autonomous drones and robots will patrol critical infrastructure perimeters and sensitive areas, especially in dangerous environments like chemical plants or power stations. Equipped with sensors, cameras, and advanced analytics, these drones will provide continuous surveillance and can respond to threats faster than humans.
- Perimeter Intrusion Detection. Advanced sensors—ranging from infrared to motion detectors and even acoustic sensors—will guard the perimeters of critical infrastructure, ensuring that any breach (physical or digital) is immediately flagged. The deployment of laser fences and sensor-embedded smart barriers could become commonplace for protecting areas like substations or pipelines.
- Biometric and Multi-factor Access Control. Future physical security systems will use multi-factor authentication (MFA), but combining biometrics with digital credentials and geo-location-based restrictions. This will make it more difficult for unauthorized personnel to gain access to restricted areas.

Technology will be at the forefront of defending critical infrastructure from the cyber perspective. We've covered these but the last one is my personal favorite:

- AI and Machine Learning. AI will play a significant role in threat detection, pattern recognition, and anomaly detection, allowing systems to react faster to attacks. However, AI-powered cyberattacks will also become more prevalent, requiring organizations to develop AI defenses that can keep up.
- IoT, IIoT and Edge Computing. As critical infrastructure incorporates more Internet of Things (IoT) devices and edge computing systems, the attack surface will expand. Securing these devices will be paramount, especially in sectors like healthcare, energy, and transportation, where IoT sensors are becoming ubiquitous.
- Blockchain. Blockchain technology will likely be used to secure the supply chains and data transactions that critical infrastructure depends on. Its decentralized and immutable nature could help prevent tampering and ensure the integrity of vital systems.
- Quantum Computing. In the future, quantum computing will pose both an opportunity and a threat. On the one hand, it could revolutionize encryption and data processing; on the other, it poses a long-term risk to current encryption standards, as quantum computers could potentially break existing cryptographic methods. There is a separate section on Quantum below, because it's THAT important. Personally speaking I can only see the threat right now, but I'm sure our species will imagineer up some opportunities when the time is right.

Governance, Risk, and Compliance (GRC)

The governance, risk, and compliance landscape will continue to evolve as regulatory bodies adapt to new security threats and best practices.

- Risk Assessments and Audits. Continuous, real-time risk assessments will be required to ensure that both

physical and cybersecurity measures are up to date. Third-party audits will become mandatory to test the robustness of security controls, with more rigorous certification requirements for companies managing critical infrastructure. Come and talk to us about our managed risk approach using ongoing risk assessment tools and other cool things.
- Stricter Regulations and Standards. Governments worldwide are likely to implement stricter regulations governing the cybersecurity of critical infrastructure, particularly after high-profile cyberattacks like the Colonial Pipeline ransomware attack in 2021. Compliance with standards like NIST (National Institute of Standards and Technology), CMMC for DoD supply chain vendors and ISO 27001 will become more rigorous, with additional scrutiny on preparedness.
- Cybersecurity Insurance. As attacks become more frequent and costly, the cyber insurance market will mature. However, insurers may demand more rigorous risk assessments and higher standards of security from organizations before offering coverage. This could drive organizations to improve their security posture to qualify for lower premiums. We have seen a trend of insurers driving up increased governance through withholding coverage. Interesting, but necessary, I think.
- Public-Private Partnerships. Governments and private sector operators of critical infrastructure will need to collaborate more closely. Programs such as CISA (Cybersecurity and Infrastructure Security Agency) in the U.S. will continue to evolve, and more resources will be dedicated to information sharing, threat intelligence, and joint response strategies.
- Risk Management Frameworks. Organizations will adopt more comprehensive risk management frameworks, incorporating both cyber and physical risks into a unified framework. This will involve regular assessments, simulations, and scenario planning to address the full spectrum of risks.

- Cross-Border Compliance. Given the global nature of critical infrastructure (e.g., international energy pipelines, global supply chains), organizations will have to navigate cross-border compliance challenges, ensuring they adhere to the regulations of multiple countries. This will require international coordination and the harmonization of cybersecurity standards.

Integration of Physical and Cybersecurity

I covered this earlier, but the future will see even more convergence of physical and cybersecurity, where the protection of critical infrastructure requires that both areas work in tandem. For instance:

- Converged Security Operations Centers (SOC). Organizations will adopt converged SOCs, where both cyber and physical security incidents are monitored and managed together. A cyber intrusion that disables physical security cameras will immediately trigger alarms in the physical security system, allowing teams to respond holistically.
- Digital Twins for Physical Security. A digital twin is a virtual representation of a physical asset. In the future, digital twins of critical infrastructure systems (like power grids, water systems, etc.) will allow organizations to simulate attacks (both physical and cyber), monitor real-time vulnerabilities, and make proactive adjustments to security postures. Over time, and with enough real-world data, AI will be able to spot trends and identify weaknesses in the security posture of a facility, and potentially automate the remediation. Or at least share those observations with other facilities for the good of the wider critical infrastructure community.

Quantum

I touched on the briefly above but wanted to get into more detail because this is going to be a game-changer. Quantum computing is poised to be one of the most transformative technologies of the 21st century, with significant implications for both physical and cybersecurity in critical infrastructure. If you can't sleep, search for quantum physics on YouTube and make yourself comfortable. Quantum computers operate fundamentally differently from classical computers, using quantum bits (qubits) that can exist in multiple states simultaneously. This allows quantum computers to process information at exponentially faster rates than today's most advanced supercomputers. While this holds great promise for innovation, it also introduces a host of new security risks.

Quantum and Physical Security

Quantum computing's impact on physical security is less direct, but there are several areas where it could enhance or undermine security for critical infrastructure:

- Quantum Sensing and Detection. Quantum technologies such as quantum sensing offer the potential to greatly enhance physical security by providing more accurate detection systems for various critical infrastructure sectors. Quantum sensors are extremely sensitive and can measure gravitational, magnetic, and electric fields with unprecedented precision. These could be used in physical security for intrusion detection, monitoring underground pipelines, or detecting movements around sensitive installations like nuclear power plants.
- Quantum radar. This technology could potentially detect stealth aircraft or drones that currently evade traditional radar systems. In the future, quantum radar might be used to protect critical airspace around power plants, government facilities, or military bases from drone attacks or other aerial threats.

- Advanced Surveillance and Imaging. Quantum-based imaging technologies, which exploit entangled photons, could allow for imaging through walls or monitoring areas without line of sight. This could be applied to enhance physical surveillance at high-security facilities, where traditional cameras and sensors may have blind spots.
- Quantum Cryptography for Secure Communications. While quantum computing threatens current encryption, quantum cryptography - specifically Quantum Key Distribution (QKD) - offers a solution to secure communication channels. QKD allows two parties to share a cryptographic key in a way that guarantees security based on the laws of physics rather than mathematical difficulty. QKD systems are already being tested in highly sensitive sectors like financial services and government communications, and critical infrastructure sectors are expected to adopt this technology to secure communication between control systems, grid operators, and remote monitoring stations.

Quantum and Cybersecurity

The most immediate concern in cybersecurity is how quantum computing will affect encryption. Current encryption algorithms, such as RSA and Elliptic Curve Cryptography (ECC), rely on the computational difficulty of factoring large numbers or solving discrete logarithms. These tasks are infeasible for classical computers to solve within a reasonable time frame, which makes them 'secure'. However, quantum computers - once fully developed - could solve these problems in minutes using Shor's algorithm, a quantum algorithm capable of efficiently breaking public-key cryptography. The potential for quantum computers to crack encryption presents a major threat to sensitive data across industries, particularly for critical infrastructure.

Key Concerns

- Breaking Public-Key Encryption. Quantum computers could render much of today's encryption obsolete. Systems that rely on RSA, ECC, or Diffie-Hellman for secure communication could be compromised, leading to the exposure of sensitive data like classified government information, financial records, and industrial control system data.
- Long-term Security Threats. Even though quantum computers capable of breaking encryption do not yet exist, adversaries could start harvesting encrypted data today, planning to decrypt it once quantum computers are available - a concept called "harvest now, decrypt later." This is particularly worrying for critical infrastructure, which stores sensitive data with long-term value, such as utility network designs, power grid control data, and military communications.

The Future – Post-Quantum Cryptography

To combat the threat of quantum computing, cryptographers are developing post-quantum cryptographic algorithms that are resistant to quantum attacks. These algorithms are based on mathematical problems that are believed to be difficult for quantum computers to solve.

National Institute of Standards and Technology (NIST) is currently working on standardizing quantum-resistant algorithms, with several candidates being tested for their robustness against quantum attacks. The implementation of post-quantum cryptography (PQC) will be essential for future-proofing critical infrastructure. Many experts believe that the first cryptographically relevant quantum computer could be developed within the next 10-20 years, making it crucial for critical infrastructure organizations to begin migrating to quantum-resistant encryption in the near future.

To my mind it looks like the future of cybersecurity in critical infrastructure will require an adaptive, resilient approach where people, processes, technology, and governance are tightly integrated. As threats grow more complex, organizations will need to invest heavily in the right technologies, while fostering a security culture that empowers employees to recognize and respond to threats. Continuous regulatory evolution, coupled with a focus on risk management and compliance, will play a crucial role in defining the security landscape for critical infrastructure in the years to come.

The future of physical security for critical infrastructure will increasingly rely on advanced technologies that integrate with digital defenses to create a unified approach to protecting critical systems. The convergence of AI, IoT, biometrics, drones, and blockchain will lead to more automated, intelligent, and proactive security solutions. Simultaneously, stricter governance, risk management, and compliance frameworks will ensure that organizations not only adopt these technologies but use them in a way that aligns with evolving security standards.

So, is the future bright, less risky, full of rainbows and unicorns? Difficult to say. The world of security, be that physical or cyber, always seems to be on the defensive against attackers. We have to learn from 'zero day' or 'original' attacks and quickly build defenses such that everyone is aware of that new attack and can defend against it. The big question mark is about Quantum computing – this is a massive double-edged sword for critical infrastructure. On one side, it presents unprecedented opportunities for secure communications and advanced detection technologies. On the other side, it threatens the cryptographic foundations upon which much of today's physical and cybersecurity systems rely.

Chapter 10 – Conclusion

It's 2024, and this is a rapidly changing landscape so all bets are off as to when this book will be redundant. Nevertheless, I see a relatively significant period of usefulness, which is why I have persevered to get this published.

If you're the sort of person that skips straight to the conclusion before reading the index, apart from being a weirdo I hope you find this list sufficiently interesting to want to flick to the front, or a chapter of your choosing. These are just a few key phrases that sprang to mind during the process:

It all starts with an assessment

It's not all about technology, it's about: People, Process, Technology, Governance, Risk, Compliance

You need a plan for everything – design, build, continuity, emergencies

You are as strong as your weakest link (this is usually a human)

Security and safety by design, not as an afterthought

(Security) culture eats strategy for breakfast (Peter Drucker, hero of mine)

Have accountability for the data

Being compliant doesn't always make you secure

Humans have to be the ultimate decision maker

Joined up thinking will serve you well, convergence is coming

Every situation is different, and so is your operating context

Doing nothing is not an option

Be afraid. (Only kidding!)

Let me take you back to the start of this book and all those dots and lines in my head. Was I able to explain my thoughts on physical and cybersecurity in the context of critical infrastructure in a way that was helpful to explain? With a bit of history, a bit of future, and few examples thrown in? Maybe the odd story?

I hope so. Thanks again to the contributors, proofreaders, and everyone who badgered me into finishing this project. I expect I went off-piste and disappeared down a few rabbit holes along the way, that's just me I'm afraid. Hope you enjoyed it, and do reach out if you need help.

Made in the USA
Columbia, SC
27 November 2024